# Contents

# About this Book

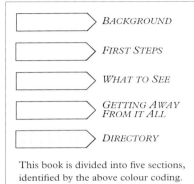

| | |
|---|---|
| | BACKGROUND |
| | FIRST STEPS |
| | WHAT TO SEE |
| | GETTING AWAY FROM IT ALL |
| | DIRECTORY |

This book is divided into five sections, identified by the above colour coding.

**Background** gives an introduction to the region – its history, geography, politics, culture.

**First Steps** offers practical advice on arriving and getting around.

**What to See** is an alphabetical listing of places to visit, interspersed with walks and tours.

**Getting Away From it All** highlights places off the beaten track where it's possible to relax and enjoy peace and quiet.

Finally, the **Directory** provides practical information – from shopping and entertainment to children and sport, including a section on business matters.

Special highly illustrated **features** on specific aspects of the region appear throughout the book.

Chatham, Cape Cod, Massachusetts

THOMAS COOK
*Travellers* & NEW ENGLAND

# BOSTON

BY
ROBERT HOLMES

Produced by AA Publishing

**Written by** Robert Holmes
**Original photography by** Robert Holmes
Edited, designed and produced by AA
Publishing. Maps © The Automobile
Association 1994, 1996, 2000

Distributed in the United Kingdom by AA
Publishing, Norfolk House, Priestley Road,
Basingstoke, Hampshire RG24 9NY.

The contents of this publication are believed
correct at the time of printing. Nevertheless, the publishers cannot
accept responsibility for any errors or omissions, or for changes in the
details given in this guide, or for the consequences of any reliance on the
information provided by the same. Assessments of attractions, hotels,
restaurants and so forth are based upon the author's own experience,
and therefore descriptions given in this guide necessarily contain an
element of subjective opinion which may not reflect the publisher's
opinion or dictate a reader's own experiences on another occasion.
**We have tried to ensure accuracy in this guide, but things do
change and we would be grateful if readers would advise us of any
inaccuracies they may encounter.**

A CIP catalogue record for this book is available from the British Library.

ISBN 0 7495 2311-5

Published by AA Publishing (a trading name of Automobile Association
Developments Limited, whose registered office is Norfolk House,
Priestley Road, Basingstoke, Hampshire RG24 9NY. Registered number
1878835) and the Thomas Cook Group Ltd.

Colour separation: BTB Colour Reproduction, Whitchurch, Hampshire.
Printed by Edicoes ASA, Oporto, Portugal.

Front cover: *Waits River, Vermont*; Back cover: *pumpkin patch; Oak
Bluffs, Massachusetts*; Title page: *Boston, Downtown from Cambridge*;
Above: *Patriot Sam Adams before Faneuil Hall*
**Cover picture credits** AA Photo Library (R. Holmes): Back cover
bottom, Spine; (M. Lynch): Back cover top; Zefa Picture Ltd: Front cover

# BACKGROUND

'Boston is a state of
mind.'
MARK TWAIN

# Introduction

*I*t may be called New England, but by American standards it is anything but new. Boston was founded 30 years before Charles II ascended to the British throne. Harvard University was in existence almost 20 years before Oliver Cromwell became the Lord Protector. This is one of the few areas of the United States steeped in history on a European scale. It is the birthplace of the present-day United States of America, and the spiritual home of the American Revolution.

New England comprises the six north-eastern states of the United States: Massachusetts, Connecticut, Vermont, New Hampshire, Maine and tiny Rhode Island. The city of Boston has always

The hamlet of East Orange, Vermont, among the gorgeous hues of the leaf-peeping season

been regarded as the region's capital.

Throughout its history, New England has always exerted an influence far greater than its size. Both Yale and Harvard are here, along with many equally prestigious seats of academia. It is home to 7.5 per cent of the nation's graduate schools, and Greater Boston alone has 65 colleges and universities.

Boston has had many of the nation's 'firsts' – among them the first public

**NEW ENGLAND**

Boston's modern skyline contrasts with the Longfellow ('Salt and Pepper') Bridge of 1900

library, public park, children's museum and computer museum – and has become a world leader in the high-technology computer industry, rivalling California's Silicon Valley in importance. Hartford, Connecticut, has long been the centre of the nation's insurance industry.

In complete contrast, the New England countryside has come to epitomise rural America – Connecticut, Rhode Island and Massachusetts being more affluent and punctuated with major urban centres, while thinly populated Vermont, New Hampshire and Maine are genuinely rural and agricultural, even relatively poor in parts. Images of white steepled churches, peeping through brilliant autumn foliage, and misty fishing harbours sheltering on a rocky coastline are as much a part of the idealised American iconography as the evocative, richly detailed paintings of Norman Rockwell, himself a New Englander (see **Stockbridge**, page 92).

This is one of the most cultural corners of America. Publishing, encouraged by the proximity of so much intellectual activity, has always thrived in the area. Many great figures of literature have made their home here, from Henry David Thoreau and Harriet Beecher Stowe to Henry Wadsworth Longfellow and Robert Frost. The museums and art galleries of Boston are world-class in both scope and importance, and the Boston Symphony is as fine an orchestra as you will find anywhere.

Whatever your interest – from nature to culture, tradition to technology – you can find it in New England.

# History

*T*he first settlers were the Algonquin Indians, who lived by hunting, fishing and raising basic crops. By the 17th century their population was already in sharp decline through disease and tribal warfare.

**1602**
Explorer Bartholomew Gosnold names Cape Cod.

**1613**
Jesuits establish a mission on Mount Desert Island, off the coast of Maine.

**1614**
The term 'New England' is used for the first time in Captain John Smith's *A Description of New England.* Smith sails into the Boston area and names the Charles River. Adrian Block, a Dutch navigator, names Block Island off the coast of Rhode Island.

**1620**
Plymouth Colony is established by Pilgrims arriving on the *Mayflower.* It is the first permanent English settlement.

**1626**
The Puritan colony of Salem is established by Roger Conant and a group of settlers.

**1630**
Boston is founded under the leadership of Puritan John Winthrop.

**1634**
Boston Common is purchased – the first public park in the USA.

**1636**
Harvard College is founded, making it America's oldest university. Roger Williams establishes Providence, Rhode Island.

**1662**
A royal charter unites the colonies of New Haven and Connecticut.

**1770**
On 5 March the Boston Massacre occurs: five colonists are killed by British bullets outside the Old State House.

**1773**
On 16 December the Boston Tea Party takes place: 342 chests of tea are tossed into Boston Harbor by colonists dressed as Indians.

**1775**
The start of the American Revolution.
*18 April* The rides of Paul Revere and William Dawes.
*19 April* Battles of Concord and Lexington.
*10 May* The siege of Fort Ticonderoga by Ethan Allen and his Green Mountain Boys.
*17 June* Battle of Bunker Hill.
*3 July* George Washington takes command of the Continental Army on Cambridge Common.

**1776**
*17 March* The British evacuate Boston.
*4 July* Declaration of Independence.

**1777**
The Battle of Bennington, Vermont. Vermont is declared an independent republic.

**1783**
The end of the American Revolution. Britain recognises independence.

**1820**
Maine becomes the 23rd state of the Union.

**1821**
The first free public school in America is opened by Horace Mann.

**1826**
Mayor Josiah Quincy starts construction

of Quincy Market by filling in the waterfront.

**1841**

Irish fleeing the potato famine start to arrive in Boston.

**1851**

Harriet Beecher Stowe starts work on her novel *Uncle Tom's Cabin* in Hartford, Connecticut.

**1852**

The first public library in America opens in Boston. The filling of Back Bay begins in Boston.

**1872**

The Great Fire destroys 770 buildings over 65 acres in the heart of the downtown area.

**1877**

The swan boats are introduced in the Public Garden.

**1897**

The first underground railway in America opens under Boston Common at Park Street.

**1910**

John F Fitzgerald, the grandfather of John F Kennedy, is elected mayor of Boston.

**1917**

John F Kennedy is born in Brookline.

**1944**

The Bretton Woods Conference is held in New Hampshire.

**1954**

The world's first atomic submarine, the *Nautilus*, is constructed at Groton, Connecticut.

**1960**

Kennedy casts his ballot in the Old West Church a few hours before being elected President.

**1976**

Quincy Market reopens after extensive restoration.

**1980**

Boston celebrates its 350th anniversary.

**1996**

The 100th Boston Marathon takes place.

Bunker Hill Monument, on Breed's Hill in Charlestown

# PILGRIMS AND PURITANS

It was a complete accident that the Pilgrims aboard the *Mayflower* landed where they did. The 102 colonists under the leadership of William Brewster had set sail from Plymouth, England, for the Virginia Colony at Jamestown, but they were blown off course. First sighting land at Cape Cod, they cruised the coast for a month until 21 December 1620, when, in search of a more hospitable environment, they crossed the bay to Plymouth. Here they established their famous settlement.

The first winter was so harsh that almost half the Pilgrims died. Friendly Indians came to the rescue with much-needed food, and in the autumn of 1621, Indian Chief Massasoit shared the original Thanksgiving feast with Governor William Bradford and the Pilgrims.

The Pilgrims were Puritans fleeing England in the wave of reform that was flowing through the church. They had deeply held religious convictions and were committed to the 'purification' of the Church of England. Persecuted

Above: the 1692 witchcraft hysteria in Salem led to the cruel deaths of 20 people
Below left: a statue of Salem's founder, Roger Conant, outside the Witch Museum

### THANKSGIVING

Celebrated on the fourth Thursday of November, Thanksgiving is a time for gathering with family and close friends to share the bounty of the harvest (these days, often timed to fit in with televised football games). Although food traditions vary around the country, the meal typically centres on turkey, cranberry sauce, cornbread and pumpkin pie – all originally from New England but adopted by Americans everywhere. The meal may resemble Christmas, but the holiday itself has a patriotic underpinning that sets it quite apart from December's festivities.

for these beliefs, they went in search of new lands where they could have the freedom to follow their ideals.

Above: the landing of the Pilgrims in 1620.
Inset: Plymouth's *Mayflower II*, a full-scale replica of the original Pilgrim vessel

More followed the *Mayflower* Pilgrims, and by 1630 the Massachusetts Bay Colony had been founded. By 1636 there were over 12,000 Puritans in settlements along the coast and in New Hampshire and Connecticut. The need for Puritan clergy resulted in the establishment of Harvard College to train future ministers.

The downfall of the Puritans was their total lack of tolerance for the beliefs of others. The Salem witch trials were a typical example of their fanaticism, but they also persecuted other religious groups, such as the Quakers, Baptists and Jews.

Roger Williams, who disagreed with this extreme attitude, was banished from the colony for his 'dangerous views'. He founded Rhode Island, which became the first state to grant complete religious freedom. Other states soon followed the same course, and long before the American Revolution, Puritanism had become a thing of the past. So precious was the principle of religious freedom that it was enshrined in the Constitution's Bill of Rights.

# Geography

*I*f geography is the shaper of human character, then New Englanders owe their formidable spirit and stubborn Yankee disposition to a landscape that is at once beautiful and harsh, generous and unforgiving. Scoured by glaciers, pounded by ocean waves and carved by an extensive system of rivers and streams, New England – the most compact region in the United States – offers a diverse landscape that seems to change with every mountain valley and sandy coastline.

The Appalachians, America's oldest mountain range, form the backbone of New England. Stretching 1,600 miles from the St Lawrence Valley in Canada to Alabama, the range branches off into two distinct New England mountain chains.

The Green Mountains form a north–south ridge that runs through the centre of the state of Vermont. Home to Vermont's rich marble deposits and the region's largest concentration of

downhill and cross-country ski resorts, they play a vital role in the state's local economy. Mount Mansfield, Vermont's tallest peak, and nearby Camels Hump are favourites among Green Mountain hikers. Lush hardwood forests yield another bounty: the sugar maple, appreciated for its colourful autumn foliage, is tapped in early spring for its

A corner of Vermont's tranquil Northeast Kingdom, famed for its Fall Foliage Festival

sap, which is boiled to make delicious maple syrup. The mountain range extends south into Massachusetts, where it is known as the Berkshire Hills.

Sculpted by receding glaciers, the spectacular White Mountains rise like sentries on the New Hampshire landscape. At 6,288 feet, Mount Washington, the highest point in the northeastern United States, is the jewel of the White Mountains. With its towering peaks, the Mount Washington Valley region inspired the White Mountains School of Art, a group of 19th-century landscape painters who brought fame to the region. Continuing north and east, the mountain chain pushes into Maine. Heading south, it links up with the Monadnocks, a series of isolated mountains that dot the landscape from southern New Hampshire into Massachusetts.

Between these mighty mountain ranges lies the Connecticut River Valley, an area of a hundred lakes, gentle hills and pristine colonial villages. Stretching 400 miles, the valley follows the course of the Connecticut River, which forms the border between Vermont and New Hampshire and divides New England in half.

As mountains give way to rolling hills, New England's character gives way to a coastline that is both harsh and inviting. The spectacular Maine coast, jagged and irregular, has an untamed feel, and was formed as glaciers retreated 11,000 years ago, leaving behind a bedrock of sandstone, limestone and shale. Here, peninsulas jut into the icy North Atlantic waters, and rocky islands with windswept pines provide a rugged retreat.

Further south, the coastal plain broadens, creating quiet lagoons and salt

Belying their name, the White Mountains shimmer with jewel-like autumn colours

marshes that are nesting grounds for a rich collection of birds and waterfowl that live along the Atlantic Flyway. These areas also provide habitats for a wide variety of flora and fauna that call New England home.

New England's most famous coastline, however, is the expanse of superb sand beaches that form the landscape of Cape Cod and the islands of Nantucket and Martha's Vineyard. These areas were formed some 100,000 years ago as a glacier pulled away, leaving behind clay, sand and rocky debris. Most of the glacial moraine formed Cape Cod, with the outermost protrusions forming the islands. Time, tides and weather have created a masterpiece along the coast: great rolling dunes, miles of white sand beaches and an austere plant life that ekes out an existence on the edge of the continent.

# Politics

*T*he birthplace of the American Revolution, New England has always been a free-thinking region where politics are a regular topic of conversation. This unfettered state of mind has created a brand of politics that holds steady in shifting political winds and exerts a powerful influence. While the rest of the country jumps on the latest bandwagon, little New England continues to declare its independence. In doing so, it reminds its fellow Americans of the core values that form the foundation of American democracy. The following is a brief look at the political history of New England, state by state:

## CONNECTICUT

Connecticut will always have a place in political history as the state where the world's first written constitution was introduced. In recent years, both in local and national politics, this has been a Democratic stronghold, although in Presidential elections, the electorate has tended to favour Republican candidates. In 1990, neither the Democrats nor Republicans dominated the state elections. The vote for Governor went to Lowell Weicker Jr, on the 'A Connecticut Party' ticket, making him one of the few independent governors ever elected. In the 1995 election the seat went to Republican John G Roland.

## MAINE

This state has been a seat of power in recent years. Former President George Bush's 'Summer White House' was located in the coastal village of Kennebunkport, and became an international centre of policy-making. Today, Maine's Democratic US Senator George Mitchell is the Senate majority leader – one of the most powerful positions in federal government.

## MASSACHUSETTS

Home to the Kennedys and long a symbol of political liberalism, Massachusetts remains an important part of the US political fabric. Boston – famous for its Irish mayors – is blessed

---

### GOVERNING BOSTON

The city of Boston is governed by a mayor, elected to a four-year term, and a city council – but it wasn't always so. Originally, Boston was a self-governing Puritan community established and run by the Massachusetts Bay Company. When the company lost its influence with the British throne, it lost its charter and Boston became part of the royal Province of Massachusetts, ruled by a Colonial governor. And so it remained – until the American Revolution. Boston was a hotbed – *the* hotbed – of Revolutionary fervour. Sam Adams and Paul Revere, the Old North Church and the Boston Tea Party are all important to the history – and mythology – of the American Revolution. The traditional town meeting, the instrument of New England democracy, soon became unwieldy. In 1822, the state granted Boston a city charter, the basis of the city's modern government.

Boston's modern Government Center contrasts with its centuries-old political heritage

with a concentration of fine universities, and these have created a climate of thinking that has inspired new ways of tackling old problems. Some of that new thinking is coming to the surface today. With the defeat of its Democratic Governor, Michael Dukakis, in the 1988 presidential elections, and the collapse of the state's economy, the Bay State cleaned house. Republican Governor William Weld, elected in 1990, is restructuring state government.

## NEW HAMPSHIRE

Over the past dozen years, few states have done more to set the terms of public debate than New Hampshire. With the lowest taxes in New England, New Hampshire has fuelled an economic resurgence and political debate. The state also wields tremendous influence in national politics. Until Bill Clinton's election in 1992, New Hampshire citizens have picked every president since 1956.

## RHODE ISLAND

This tiny state has been a supporter of the Democratic Party since the 1930s, but charges of corruption and a destabilisation of the state economy have weakened support. Rhode Island is one of two states with no county government. It is divided into 39 municipalities, each with its own form of local government.

## VERMONT

To many, Vermont represents the future of American politics. The state's strong tradition of local government – typified by annual town meetings where budgets are determined by public hearings – has caught the imagination of both the public and politicians alike. With its Yankee heritage, it was long the most Republican state in the country. Yet today Vermont boasts some of the nation's leading environmental policies; it also has America's only Socialist Congressman, Bernard Sanders.

# Culture

*T*he original Indian tribes of New England – the Penobscot, Passamaquoddy, Wampanoag and Mashpee – have all but disappeared. As happened all over America, they were wiped out either by warfare, or by disease introduced by the settlers. The final blow was the result of a 'war' started by an Indian named Philip. Concerned about the growing dominance of the whites, he persuaded several tribes to band together to fight the English. 'King Philip', as the Colonists called him, was betrayed and King Philip's War broke out in 1675. By the time he was killed in 1676, the Indian population had been virtually exterminated. The few native Americans that remain today live on reservations in Maine, Cape Cod and Martha's Vineyard.

Until the mid-1800s most of the population were descendants of the British Puritans. These Yankees were hard-working and adaptable. Their renowned ingenuity gave New England a tremendous boost during the Industrial Revolution. Several inventions, such as the cotton gin, established New England as the industrial centre of the nation. The great Irish potato famine of 1845 resulted in an enormous influx of Irish immigrants attracted by the wealth of New England and the availability of jobs. Lithuanians, Poles, Germans and Russian Jews followed. The Italians came in the 1870s and, later, French Canadians – all in search of work.

In Boston, the black community that lived in the North End was replaced by the Irish, then by the Jews and finally by the Italians, who remain there to this day. The blacks moved to Beacon Hill before finally settling in the larger cities of southern New England. Beacon Hill became, and still is, a quarter for the social aristocracy, nicknamed the 'Boston Brahmins'. These wealthy, white Anglo-Saxons constitute America's nearest equivalent to the British upper class.

THOMAS COOK'S NEW ENGLAND
*The first Cook's tour to the New England states was led by John Mason Cook, son of Thomas, in 1866. He travelled on the Inman Line steamer* City of Boston *from Liverpool to New York. After a few days in that city the party set off on the Hudson River line to such towns as Albany and Troy. Later tours included Boston and after the Cooks became partners of Jenkins, the business developed rapidly with tours all over America.*

**YANKEE**
No one really knows where the term 'Yankee', for a New Englander, came from. Some claim it is a corruption of the Native American word for English, but many think it is derived from the Dutch – *Janke* was used as a derisive nickname by the Dutch and English for New Englanders.

# *FIRST STEPS*

'We say cows laid out
Boston. Well, there are
worse surveyors.'
RALPH WALDO EMERSON,
1860

# First Steps

New England is in many ways the most European of the American regions. It has history, the architecture is usually of European derivation, and the people tend to have a European temperament.

## Proud traditionalists

New Englanders tend to be more reserved than the average American and more in love with tradition. You will find in Boston America's closest equivalent to the British class system. For a start there is a distinct Boston accent, which many Americans consider 'refined'. Then there are the 'Boston Brahmins', a name coined by Oliver Wendell Holmes back in the 19th century. These were originally the wealthy merchants of the city, almost always descendants of the early Puritan settlers. They were well-educated (usually at Harvard), well-read, well-travelled and very conservative. As the old saying goes, 'The Lowells talk only to the Cabots, and the Cabots talk only to God.'

This attitude persists down to this day and can be encountered in institutions like the Boston Athenaeum.

The Daughters of the American Revolution (DAR) is typical of the organisations that still have a very loyal and active membership. Exclusive men's clubs are also a Boston tradition, though times are changing a little, and most of them now have to admit women to membership.

Today, it is fair to say that only a tiny minority cling to the old elitist attitude. One reason for this is that, as other ethnic groups came over to the New World, the population became much more diverse. The 'proper Bostonian' is alive and well but rarely found outside of Boston. Only Newport, Rhode Island, attracts a similar strata of society.

Other areas of New England are much more relaxed and informal. The whole of the northern area, including the states of Vermont, New Hampshire and Maine, is very rural and, while the people have an easy-going attitude to life, they remain fiercely independent.

## Driving

For most visitors the first contact comes after picking up a car at the airport, although in Boston itself a car is a definite handicap. At Boston's Logan Airport the city is so close that it's better to jump straight into a taxi and head for the hotel. But as soon as you leave the city, a car will be a necessity. Public transport basically does not exist outside the cities. New England is a compact

The best way to tour New England is by car

area and is both quick and easy to get around – but not without a car.

Driving is on the right, and though the freeway traffic may appear intimidating, no one goes very fast.

One disturbing aspect of freeway travel is that people overtake on both sides. There is theoretically a fast lane, but it's not unheard of to find someone in it pottering along at 40mph. Fortunately lane discipline is very good, but remember to keep your eyes open and use your mirrors frequently.

In late 1995, the power to impose speed limits was handed from the Federal government to the individual states. Many states have raised the speed limit on freeways to 70mph but it is still a transitional period at the time of writing. To avoid confusion, follow the clearly posted speed limit signs. Speeding tickets are very expensive, so take care. Patrol cars operate on the freeways, and radar traps are frequently used in towns and cities. Drink-driving laws are extremely tough.

**Parking**

Although, or maybe because, the car is such a major part of life in America, looking for a parking space, particularly in city centres, can be like searching for the Holy Grail.

Street parking is generally regulated by meters, with time limits ranging from 15 minutes to 4 hours. The majority of meters allow 1-hour parking and they almost all accept quarters (25-cent coins). The most expensive meters in major city centres cost $1 for 30 minutes. Feeding meters is prohibited, but it is nevertheless a common practice.

If a meter is obviously out of order, the usual solution is to write 'Meter Broken' on a paper grocery bag and

Just joking (you hope!) in Boston's North End

place it over the meter. This will usually prevent a parking ticket.

Always read notices attached to meters. On major streets in cities, parking is often restricted at peak commuting times. The most common hours are 7–9am and 4–6pm, and during these periods you will not only get a hefty parking ticket, but also have your car towed away at considerable additional expense.

A 'wheelchair' symbol indicates a zone exclusively reserved for handicapped motorists. Do not park in these zones – they carry the highest parking penalty.

All streets without meters are available for parking unless otherwise posted, but remember to park in the direction of the traffic.

In most towns, parking is prohibited for a couple of hours one day of the week for street cleaning. This can be almost any time of the day or night, so read the small print on street signs.

# BOSTON SUBWAY

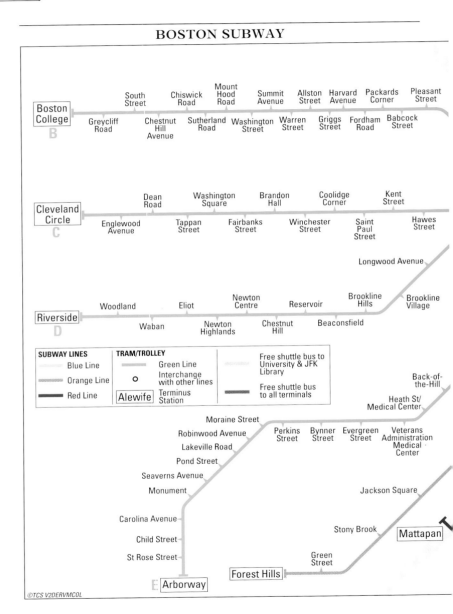

**Boston College** · B
Greycliff Road · South Street · Chestnut Hill Avenue · Chiswick Road · Sutherland Road · Mount Hood Road · Washington Street · Summit Avenue · Warren Street · Allston Street · Griggs Street · Harvard Avenue · Fordham Road · Packards Corner · Babcock Street · Pleasant Street

**Cleveland Circle** · C
Englewood Avenue · Dean Road · Tappan Street · Washington Square · Fairbanks Street · Brandon Hall · Winchester Street · Coolidge Corner · Saint Paul Street · Kent Street · Hawes Street

Longwood Avenue

**Riverside** · D
Woodland · Waban · Eliot · Newton Centre · Newton Highlands · Chestnut Hill · Reservoir · Beaconsfield · Brookline Hills · Brookline Village

## SUBWAY LINES
Blue Line
Orange Line
Red Line

## TRAM/TROLLEY
Green Line
○ Interchange with other lines
Alewife Terminus Station

Free shuttle bus to University & JFK Library
Free shuttle bus to all terminals

Back-of-the-Hill
Heath St/ Medical Center

Moraine Street
Robinwood Avenue
Lakeville Road
Pond Street
Seaverns Avenue
Monument

Perkins Street · Bynner Street · Evergreen Street · Veterans Administration Medical Center

Jackson Square

Carolina Avenue
Child Street
St Rose Street

Stony Brook

**Mattapan**

Green Street

**Forest Hills**

E · **Arborway**

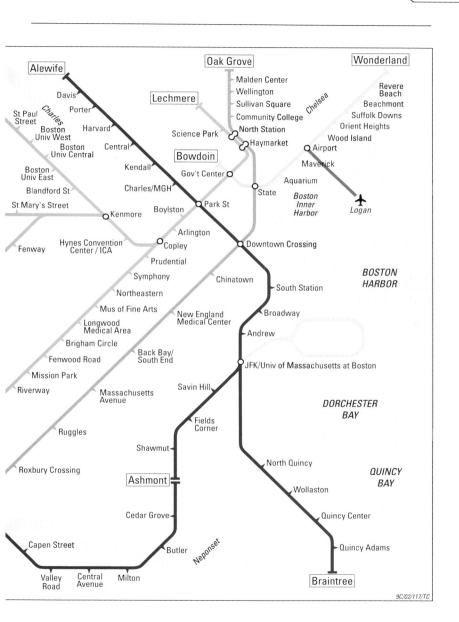

Alewife

Davis
Porter
St Paul
Street
Charles
Boston
Univ West
Harvard
Boston
Univ Central
Central
Boston
Univ East
Kendall
Charles/MGH
Blandford St
St Mary's Street
Kenmore
Boylston
Fenway
Hynes Convention
Center / ICA
Copley
Arlington
Prudential
Symphony
Northeastern
Mus of Fine Arts
Longwood
Medical Area
Brigham Circle
Fenwood Road
Mission Park
Riverway
Massachusetts
Avenue
Ruggles
Roxbury Crossing

Oak Grove

Malden Center
Wellington
Sullivan Square
Community College
North Station
Haymarket

Lechmere

Science Park

Bowdoin

Gov't Center
Park St
State
Downtown Crossing

Wonderland

Revere
Beach
Beachmont
Suffolk Downs
Orient Heights
Wood Island
Airport
Maverick
Aquarium

Chelsea

Boston
Inner
Harbor

Logan

Chinatown
New England
Medical Center
Back Bay/
South End

South Station
Broadway
Andrew
JFK/Univ of Massachusetts at Boston

BOSTON
HARBOR

Savin Hill

DORCHESTER
BAY

Fields
Corner

Shawmut

Ashmont

Cedar Grove

Capen Street

Butler

Neponset

Valley
Road
Central
Avenue
Milton

North Quincy
Wollaston

Quincy Center

Quincy Adams

Braintree

QUINCY
BAY

9C/02/117/TC

Step into yesteryear: a shop in Peacham, Vermont, invites serious browsing

### Service and shops

Most visitors are impressed with the quality of service in New England. Restaurant staff are nearly always polite and efficient, and even the conventional send-off of 'Have a nice day' is more often meant than not. There is a reason for this. Americans expect tips. It is normal to leave 15 per cent of the total bill in restaurants, more if the service has been above average.

Service standards are generally high, and there is a strong work ethic. Shops are open late and some never close (although in the more rural areas of New England there may only be one general store in the village, and it is unlikely to stay open late). Most major super-markets are open until at least 10pm and often until midnight. The 7–11 chain of convenience stores never closes at all, and they can be found open in most larger towns, 365 days of the year. They stock a basic range of foodstuffs and also serve coffee and some fast foods. Even the big department stores open late at least one night a week, and all but the smallest shops are open on Sundays.

Sales are a way of life here, and most weeks one store or another will be having one. Filene's Basement in Boston is one permanent sale that has become a New England institution. The prices can sometimes be unbelievably low, and, depending on foreign exchange rates, incredible bargains can be found. Local newspapers always carry advertisements with details.

Remember that if a state charges sales tax, it is always *added* to the marked price. Nothing is more frustrating than waiting in a long queue at a cash register to find that the item you thought you had just enough money to buy has an additional 5 to 7 per cent added. The exact rate will depend on the state you are in (New Hampshire has no sales tax).

### The recession

New England is still a relatively rich region, but the global recession of recent years has certainly had a massive impact. Property prices have plummeted and there is an increasing homeless problem in the big cities. However, the biggest effect on visitors is that many attractions that have been around for years are suddenly going out of business, and those that remain open have severely curtailed their opening times. Always telephone ahead to check the current situation.

# WHAT TO SEE

'Crush up a sheet of letter-
paper in your hand,
throw it down, stamp it
flat, and that is
a map of old Boston'
WALT WHITMAN, 1882

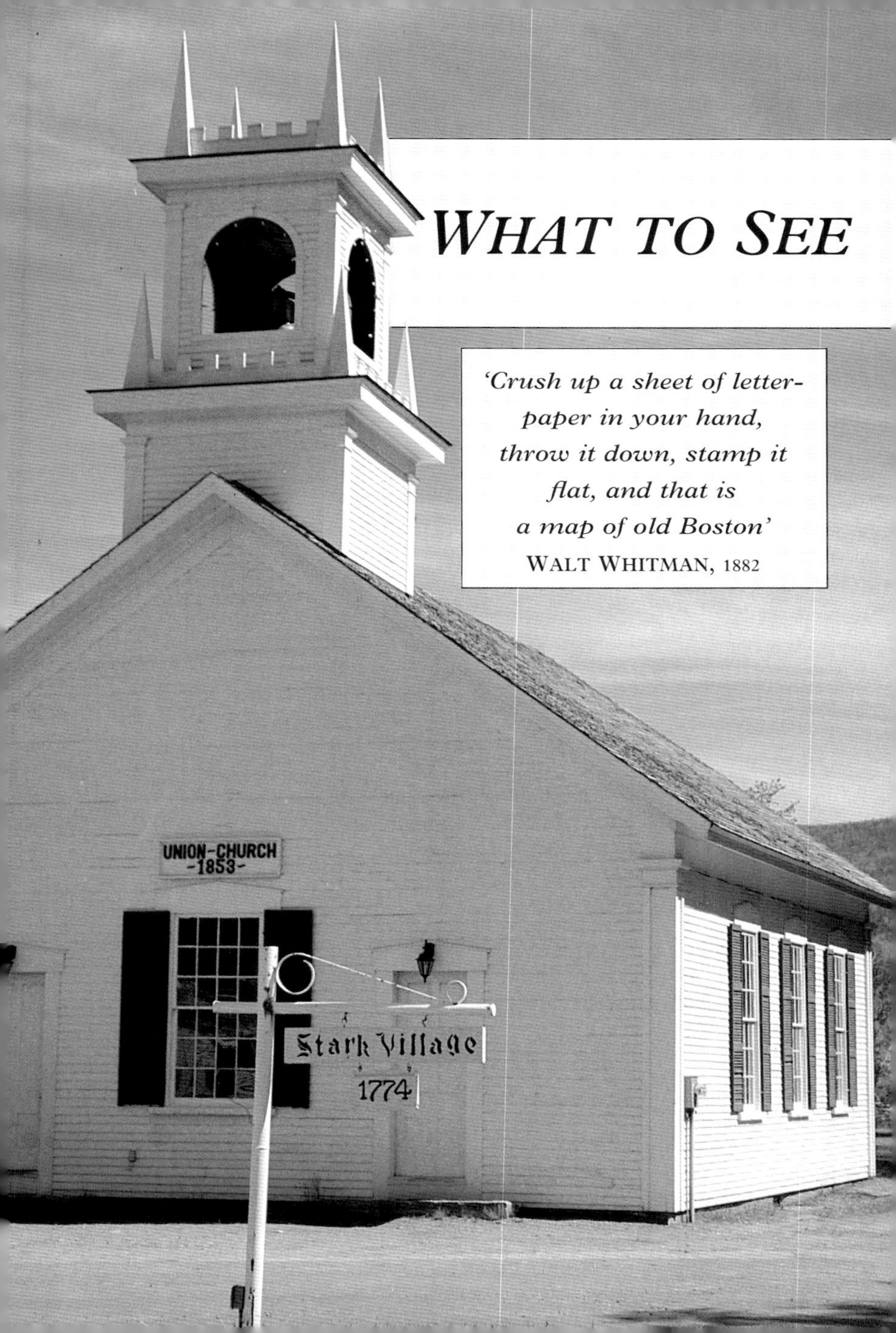

UNION-CHURCH
-1853-

Stark Village
1774

# Boston

*B*oston, the cosmopolitan capital of Massachusetts, is the most European of American cities. In spite of its population (Boston is the seventh largest city in the United States, with over 2 million), it is quite compact and is one of the very few American cities in which walking is a delight. Most of the major sights are within walking distance of each other, and the public transport system is excellent. The underground railway, the MBTA (popularly referred to as the T), covers the whole of the greater Boston area speedily, cleanly, efficiently and safely. Logan Airport is located closer to the downtown area than any other airport serving a major American city.

In America, Boston is second only to San Francisco in popularity with tourists. A recent survey in a major American travel magazine placed Boston as the seventh most popular city in the world, surpassed only by Paris, London, Rome, Vienna, Venice and San Francisco.

What accounts for such popularity? One reason, surely, is the tangible sense of history in Boston (one of the few major American cities that can make such a claim). It is in many ways the birthplace of the United States.

The museums and art galleries have world-class collections, and a visit to the city could be devoted to these alone. In Boston the visitor is offered everything from the finest dining to shopping that ranges from great bargains to the ultimate in chic.

Beyond all of this, Boston is the gateway to New England – a region of unique beauty and charm.

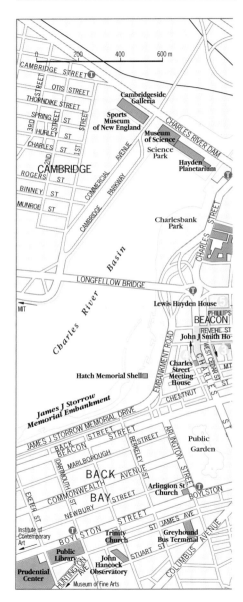

# BOSTON

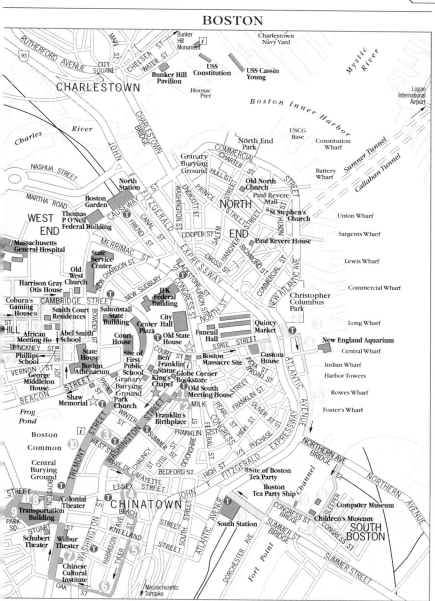

memorabilia of early telephone history.
*185 Franklin Street. Tel: (617) 743–9800.*
*Open: during normal office hours. Free.*
*T station: Downtown Crossing.*

### ARNOLD ARBORETUM

Out on Boston's Jamaica Plain, this 265-acre park forms a major link in the city's 'Emerald Necklace'. Established in 1872, it contains over 7,000 varieties of trees and plants from around the world. The self-guided walks are recommended (maps from the Visitor Center).
*125 Arborway, Jamaica Plain. Tel: (617) 524–1718; (617) 524–1717 for blossom information. Open: Monday to Friday 9am–4pm, weekends 10am–4pm. Free.*

### BEACON HILL

Beacon Hill lies to the northwest of Boston Common and slopes down to the Charles River. The name was derived from the light used in 1634 to warn colonial settlers of danger. Now it is an exclusive residential area topped by the golden-domed State House. There is no more charming area in Boston than the Hill, and it has been a much sought-after address for over two centuries. The atmosphere is typically English, with red-brick mansions and narrow cobblestone streets – so English, in fact, that film companies often use the area as a location to represent old London.

A good introduction to Beacon Hill is the Black Heritage Trail (see pages 48–9), but there are some worthwhile interesting detours.

**Acorn Street**, off West Cedar Street, is a picture-perfect, narrow cobblestone street that was originally the home of servants to the nearby mansions.

### ALEXANDER GRAHAM BELL EXHIBIT

In the heart of downtown Boston, in the New England Telephone Building, is one of the smallest museums you will find anywhere. A dark, cupboard-like room just off the entrance lobby houses a detailed reconstruction of the attic where the first electrical transmission of speech over a wire marked the birth of the telephone on 3 June 1875.

The original building occupied by Alexander Graham Bell – one of the most prolific inventors of the 19th century – was demolished in the late 1920s, but each piece of wood from the attic was removed, numbered and noted on precise plans, then reassembled in its present location in 1959. The diorama seen from the window depicts Boston as it looked in 1875. Exhibits display the first telephone switchboard, the first commercial telephone and other

It is perhaps the most photographed street in Boston, benefiting greatly from the ban on parking. Across Mount Vernon Street is exclusive **Louisburg Square** with its private central park. The 19th-century author Louisa May Alcott (*Little Women*) lived at no 10, and the square is still considered the best address in Boston.

At 55 Mount Vernon Street, the **Nichols House Museum** is a good example of a 19th-century row (terraced) house. Rose Standish Nichols was a pioneer landscape architect and peace advocate, and the niece of sculptor Augustus Saint-Gaudens. The house is full of *memorabilia*, sculptures and antique furnishings (tel: 617 227–6993 for opening times).

Harrison Gray Otis was a larger-than-life developer who also became Mayor of Boston and a member of the Senate. He had three houses built in Boston, all designed by his friend Charles Bulfinch. His second house, at 85 Mount Vernon Street, was one of the biggest on the Hill at the time, but he soon moved on to 45 Beacon Street. Also worth noting in Beacon Street are the **Appleton-Parker Houses** at 39–40. These two identical buildings were designed for a pair of wealthy merchants in the Greek Revival style. Number 39 witnessed the marriage of Fanny Appleton to Henry Wadsworth Longfellow in 1843. Notice the purple window panes. Shipments of glass sent from Hamburg to Boston between 1818 and 1824 contained magnesium, which turned the glass purple in the New England sunlight. These are some of the only authentic examples of Beacon Hill glass that remain.

*T Station: Park Street.*

Park alongside the Charles River

## BOSTON ATHENAEUM

Visitors are tolerated rather than welcomed at this bastion of Old Boston. Founded in 1807, the dark and foreboding exterior of this private library reflects the less than warm welcome waiting inside. However, the building is a National Historic Landmark and is well worth visiting. Architecturally, the interior is splendid with high, vaulted ceilings and dozens of marble busts in pillared archways. It was the home of Boston's first fine art gallery and it still houses an impressive collection of paintings by such artists as John Singer Sargent and Gilbert Stuart. Visitors are allowed to tour the library, which includes the private library of George Washington.

The leather-chaired Reading Room on the fifth floor is the most splendid in the Athenaeum. The balcony outside offers a superb view of the Old Granary Burying Ground.

*10½ Beacon Street. Tel: (617) 227–0270. Open: Monday 9am–8pm, Tuesday to Friday 9am–5.30pm, Saturday 9am–4pm. Tours: Tuesday and Thursday. Closed: July – mid-September. Free. T station: Park Street.*

## BOSTON COMMON

In the very heart of Boston is a 50-acre parcel of land that has been a public park since 1634, making it the oldest in the country. Originally the land was used for grazing sheep and cattle, and even as a military training ground. Now it is the ideal place to stroll. Musicians, jugglers, orators and puppeteers are just a few of the many diversions to watch on

The Boston Tea Party Ship, where history lives aboard this 1908 Danish replica

a sunny afternoon in the park. Sadly, like urban parks everywhere, this is not a safe place to be at night.
*T station: Park Street and Boylston.*

## BOSTON GLOBE TOURS

The *Boston Globe* is one of America's most respected daily newspapers, and free tours are offered to anyone wishing to see how a major newspaper works, including the printing presses (no children under 12). The *Globe* building is not far from the JFK Library and Museum, and a combined visit avoids having to make two trips to this outpost in south Boston.
*135 Morrissey Boulevard, Dorchester. Tel: (617) 929–2653. Open Tuesday and Thursday. T station: JFK/U Mass.*

## BOSTON MASSACRE SITE

The site of the Boston Massacre – where five Patriots were killed by British troops in 1770 – is marked by a small ring of stones embedded in the pavement in State Street, just in front of the Old State House. It is very easy to miss in the midst of the surrounding modern commercial buildings.
*T station: State.*

## BOSTON PUBLIC LIBRARY

America's finest talents were brought together to build the most magnificent library in the land – architects McKim, Mead and White, painters John Singer Sargent, Edwin Abbey and Puvis de Chavannes, and sculptors Bela Pratt, Augustus Saint-Gardens and Daniel Chester French. On completion in 1895, it admirably lived up to its name as a 'Palace for the People'. Although somewhat faded, it is still a fine example of lavish municipal architecture. Look for the murals by Sargent and linger in

Boston Common, with the golden-domed State House behind, once witnessed executions

the Italianate central courtyard.
*666 Boylston Street (at Dartmouth Street). Tel: (617) 536–5400. Open: Monday to Thursday 9am–9pm, Friday and Saturday 9am–5pm. Free tours on Friday and Saturday 11am, closed Sunday in summer T Station: Copley/Back Bay*

## BOSTON TEA PARTY SHIP

A replica of one of the three original two-masted Danish brigs sits close to the 1773 site of the Boston Tea Party. Costumed sailors act as guides, and you can even throw a bale of tea over the side (it is hauled back up again by an attached rope). An adjacent museum has an audio-visual presentation describing the events leading up to the Tea Party (see pages 32 and 53).
*Congress Street Bridge. Tel: (617) 338–1773. Open: daily 9am–dusk. Admission charge. T station: South Station.*

Take the wheel of the proud *Constitution*, saved from the scrap yard back in 1830

## BULL AND FINCH PUB

Every day of the week people can be seen queuing for hours to enter this basement bar and restaurant. It is a curious phenomenon. The scriptwriters for the popular television programme called *Cheers* loosely based their series on the Bull and Finch. The exterior is shown briefly at the beginning of each episode, but the interior bears no relationship to the television stage set. Such is the power of TV in America that the pub attracts scores of pilgrims every day, but no one seems too disappointed at the difference. The bar food, in any case, is quite good, and there is plenty of atmosphere if you can manage to avoid the crowds.

*84 Beacon Street. Tel: (617) 227–9605. Open: daily 11am–2 am. T station: Arlington.*

## BUNKER HILL MONUMENT

It was at Bunker Hill in 1775 that patriot Colonel William Prescott issued the famous command not to fire 'till you see the whites of their eyes'. Although the Redcoats ultimately seized the hill, over 1,000 British soldiers were killed in the battle, and the massive casualties were a severe blow. The battle is re-enacted annually on 17 June by costumed soldiers.

The monument, a 220-foot obelisk of granite from the nearby town of Quincy, has 295 steps leading to an observatory which has sweeping views of Charlestown and the navy yard, with Boston in the distance. At the foot of the monument is a small museum, The Lodge, with dioramas of the battle and weapons demonstrations during the summer.

*Monument Square, Charlestown. Tel: (617) 242–5641. Open: daily 9am–5pm (museum), 9am–4.30pm (monument). Closed: Thanksgiving, Christmas and New Year's Day. Free. Take the Orange Line to Haymarket T station, then bus 93 to Bunker Hill.*

## CHARLESTOWN NAVY YARD

The navy yard's 30-acre site is part of the Boston National Historic Park. The yard was opened in 1800 to build and maintain ships for the US Navy, and it finally closed in 1974. The centrepiece of the site is the world's oldest commissioned warship still afloat. The USS *Constitution* – nicknamed 'Old Ironsides' – was built in 1794. It destroyed or captured 42 enemy ships, but was never defeated in battle. The public can go on board the ship.

Also in the yard is the USS *Constitution* Museum, which interprets the *Constitution*'s history and the

Detail of 'Old Ironsides', so nicknamed when British cannonballs bounced off her oak hull

country's Federal period. The museum has several interactive exhibits and a resident model maker. The USS *Cassin Young*, a World War II destroyer, is also on exhibit in the yard.

*Charlestown Navy Yard. Tel: (617) 242–5601. Open: daily 9am–5pm, 9am–6pm during summer. Closed Thanksgiving, Christmas and New Year's Day. Free, except for the museum.*

## CHILDREN'S MUSEUM

A giant milk bottle, now a Boston landmark, sits at the end of Congress Street Bridge on Museum Wharf. The bottle has been an outdoor refreshment stand since it was donated to the Children's Museum in 1977, and behind it is one of the most ambitious and extensive children's museums in the country. Four floors of exhibits cater for children of all ages, from toddlers to teenagers and beyond. Most of the exhibits are hands-on and all offer learning and cultural experiences. There is an authentic Japanese silk merchant's house from Kyoto to explore, an exhibit on multi-culturalism that was the first of its kind, a 'Grandmother's Attic' where

Vintage kitsch outside the Children's Museum: this 1930s lunch stand is 40 feet tall

children can dress up in vintage clothes, and an extensive programme of special exhibits, events and performances (see page 53).

*300 Congress Street. Tel: (617) 426–8855. Open: daily 10am–5pm, Friday till 9pm. Closed: Monday, also Thanksgiving, Christmas and New Year's Day. Admission charge . T station: South Station.*

# The Revolution

*F*or years prior to the War of Independence, unrest and resistance to authority had been growing in Britain's North American colonies. Increasing taxes and trade restrictions, combined with no right to representation in Parliament, became a burden the Colonials were increasingly unwilling to bear. When a stamp tax was imposed in 1765, a group of Patriots formed the 'Sons of Liberty', dedicated to freeing America from Britain.

In 1770, in the now-occupied city of Boston, a belligerent mob was fired upon by British troops, and five Colonists were killed. The Boston Massacre, as it was soon called, was an indication of the violence to come.

Four years later, in 1774, a tax on tea pushed the Patriots over the edge. One dark December night a group of 200 Boston merchants disguised themselves as Indians, boarded British ships and quietly dumped 342 chests of tea into Boston Harbor. This 'Boston Tea Party' had grave consequences: the port was closed, the city was placed under martial law, and fresh British troops were quartered in private homes. A few months later, concerned at the growing atmosphere of rebelliousness, the general in charge of British forces in Boston decided on a show of force to overawe the Colonials. Seven hundred British regulars were ordered to march the 20 miles to Concord to seize illegal rebel military stores.

But the Patriots were unexpectedly well-organised. Two signal lanterns placed in the steeple of Boston's Old North Church told Paul Revere that the British were setting out for their Concord raid by boat from Boston Common. Revere then began his famous midnight ride to Concord to warn the Patriots to prepare for battle.

When, on their way to Concord, the Redcoats arrived at Lexington early on the morning of 19 April 1775, they were met by a group of about 77 Minutemen – members of the citizen army who volunteered to be ready to fight at a minute's notice. The outcome was an easy victory for the British, who then marched the 5 miles to Concord. There they met hundreds more Minutemen. The North Bridge was the site of 'the shot heard round the world' – the first shot fired by an American in the War of Independence. The Redcoats began their return march around noon along Battle Road and were joined by 1,000 reinforcements at Lexington. Only this saved the British from complete disaster in their retreat back to Boston, through what now amounted to thousands of armed and determined Colonials.

George Washington was appointed to command the army of the Continental

Minuteman at the Minuteman National Historic Park

Congress two months later on 15 June, and the first great battle of the war took place just two days later on Breed's Hill north of Boston. After desperate fighting on both sides, the Americans fell back, defeated, to nearby Bunker Hill. In spite of this, the Americans considered the 'Battle of Bunker Hill' almost a moral victory, as their amateur, half-disciplined army of citizens had inflicted heavy losses on professional British troops, a high proportion of them officers.

Fighting continued south of New England in the mid-Atlantic and southern colonies, and in the midst of this the Declaration of Independence was issued on 4 July 1776. The Revolutionary War was a long, drawn-out struggle which, in theory, the British should have won – and nearly did. But the decisive battle came in October 1781 at Yorktown, Virginia, when General Washington defeated General Cornwallis with the aid of the French, America's

Re-enacting history on the Old North Bridge

allies throughout the conflict. This victory ended the war, although British troops stayed on American soil for two more years before the Treaty of Paris, signed in September 1783, recognised American independence.

The Tea Party lives on in Boston Harbor

Even the telephone booths look the part in Boston's colourful Chinatown

## CHINATOWN

Chinatown lies immediately to the southeast of Boston Common adjoining the theatre district. Although rather small compared to other American Chinatowns, it is nevertheless

The 670-foot-long reflecting pool of the Christian Science complex covers a garage

authentically Chinese. The telephone booths are covered with pagodas, street signs are in Chinese, and the neighbourhood is entered through a massive gate that was a Bicentennial gift from Taiwan. There is no shortage of restaurants, shops selling all manner of Chinese foods and spices, and even crates of live chickens for sale. The Chinese Cultural Institute, at 276 Tremont Street, has regular exhibits of Chinese arts and crafts, together with concerts and dramatic productions. Chinatown, unfortunately, rubs shoulders with Boston's seamy side, and 'adult' establishments spill over into this otherwise interesting neighbourhood. *T station: Chinatown.*

## CHRISTIAN SCIENCE CENTER

Boston is the world headquarters of the Christian Science religion, founded by Mary Baker Eddy in 1879. A harmonious group of buildings has developed close to the Prudential Center. The original Mother Church, (1894), was gradually joined by other buildings, culminating in the pedestrian plaza and reflecting pool. By far the most interesting exhibit at the Center is a 30-foot stained-glass walk-through globe, called the Mapparium, representing the world as it looked in 1935. Tour groups tend to visit in the mornings, so it may be better to avoid this time. A small window at the side gives a good view without having to wait. The globe is housed in the Publishing Society Building, home of the *Christian Science Monitor*.
*175 Huntington Avenue. Tel: (617) 450–2000. Open: May to October, Tuesday to Saturday 9am–4pm, Sunday 11.15am–4pm. November to April, Tuesday to Saturday 10am–4pm, Sunday 11.15am–2pm. Free. T station: Symphony and Prudential.*

## COMPUTER MUSEUM

This is the only museum in the world dedicated solely to computers. Many of the displays are interactive, and the computer fanatic will be able to spend hours playing in the technocrats toy shop. A giant two-storey walk-through model computer is the central focus of the museum, and this is continually updated to keep pace with the latest advances in technology (see page 53).
*300 Congress Street (Museum Wharf). Tel: (617) 426–2800. Open: daily 10am–5pm. Closed: Monday (September through June), Thanksgiving, Christmas, New Year's Day. Admission charge. T station: South Station.*

## COPP'S HILL BURYING GROUND

Boston's second oldest cemetery, dating back to 1659, played a significant role in the battle for independence. The British placed several guns here to fire on the Americans during the Battle of Bunker Hill, but to little effect. More devastating was the attack on Charlestown with incendiary shells. The British used the gravestones for target practice, and you can still see the marks left by musket balls on the gravestones of Grace Berry and Daniel Malcolm.
*Hull and Snowhill Streets. No convenient T station.*

## FANEUIL HALL

The gold-plated grasshopper weathervane, modelled after a similar weathervane on London's Royal Exchange, has been spinning on top of Faneuil Hall since 1742. The hall was originally built as a market, but became known as the 'Cradle of Liberty' because of the patriotic speeches by Samuel Adams and James Otis at town meetings held on the upper floors.

The assembly room on the first floor is still used for town meetings, and it is worth a visit to view Daniel Healy's huge painting, *Liberty and Union, Now and Forever*, which dominates the room. On the top floor is the military museum and headquarters of the Ancient and Honorable Artillery Company of Massachusetts, America's oldest military organisation, chartered in 1638. National Park rangers give interpretative talks in the hall throughout the day.

Immediately behind Faneuil Hall is Quincy Market, a lively collection of eating places and shops, and one of the most popular attractions in the country.
*Congress Street. Tel: (617) 338–2323. Open: Monday to Saturday 10am–9pm, Sunday noon–7pm. Free. T station: Government Center/Haymarket. Quincy Market open as above.*

The 4-foot gilt-copper grasshopper atop Faneuil Hall is an 18th-century weathervane

## GIBSON HOUSE

Although this is one of the city's least-known museums, it gives the most complete picture of Victorian Boston. The house was built in Back Bay for Catherine Hammond Gibson in 1859, and it passed through three generations of this prominent Boston family before being opened as a museum in 1957. The house is a perfectly preserved Victorian time capsule full of absolutely authentic furniture, possessions and decorations. Not only can you experience the cluttered opulence of upper-class Boston, but also tour downstairs, the kitchen, pantries and laundry. Tours start promptly; even if you are only a couple of minutes late, you will not be allowed inside.

Time to reflect on God and Mammon: Trinity Church dominated by the Hancock Tower

*137 Beacon Street. Tel: (617) 267–6338. Open: May to October, Wednesday to Sunday; November to April, Saturday and Sunday. Tours start precisely at 1, 2 and 3pm. Closed: major holidays. Admission charge. T station: Arlington.*

## GLOBE CORNER BOOKSTORE

During the mid-19th century the Old Corner Bookstore (now restored and renamed) was the literary hub of Boston (see page 46). Writers including Longfellow, Hawthorne and Emerson would regularly meet here, and both Charles Dickens and William Makepeace Thackeray stopped by on their visits to America. During this period, Tickner and Fields published works by Harriet Beecher Stowe, Thoreau, Browning, Julia Ward Howe, Emerson and many other prominent local authors, helping to establish a body of North American literature. Once threatened by urban renewal, it was saved by preservationists. In 1982 it was reopened as a travel bookstore, with a good selection of books on New England and works by New England authors. *500 Boylston Street. Tel: (617) 859–8008. Open: Monday to Friday 9.30am–8pm, Saturday 9.30am–7pm, Sunday noon–6pm. T station: State.*

## INSTITUTE OF CONTEMPORARY ART

Housed in an old fire station, this Romanesque-style building hosts revolving exhibits on the cutting edge of modern art. The mixed media, video, performance and music events are often controversial and always stimulating. There is no permanent collection. *955 Boylston Street. Tel: (617) 266–5152 for opening hours. T station: Hynes Convention Center.*

## ISABELLA STEWART GARDNER MUSEUM

This unusual and delightful museum, housed in a replica of a 15th-century Venetian palace, contains the personal collection of Isabella Stewart Gardner, amassed on her travels to Europe. The eclectic collection was personally arranged by Mrs Gardner, resulting in some bizarre and idiosyncratic displays. When she died in 1924, she willed that if anything was rearranged, then the entire contents of the museum should be sold and the monies given to Harvard University (fortunately nothing has been touched!). The galleries, containing a priceless collection of fine and applied arts, all open on to a central courtyard full of greenery and fountains. All the great masters are represented here, with paintings by Rembrandt, Titian, Vermeer, Rubens, Raphael, Botticelli, Manet, Matisse and the only fresco by Piero della Francesca outside Italy. From September to June classical concerts are held in the Tapestry Room three times a week.
*280 The Fenway. Tel: (617) 566–1401; (617) 734–1359 for concert information. Open: Tuesday to Sunday 11am–5pm. Closed: Monday, national holidays. Admission charge. T station: Museum of Fine Arts.*

## JOHN HANCOCK OBSERVATORY/PRUDENTIAL TOWER SKY WALK

The best view of Boston is from the 60th floor of the tallest building in New England. I M Pei designed the 740-foot-high John Hancock Observatory in the late 1960s, and the 13 acres of mirror-glass walls have become a well-known city landmark. Adjacent to the Hancock is a topographical model of Boston as it was in 1775, complete with a sound and

The graceful arches and formal plantings of the courtyard in the Gardner Museum

light show depicting the events of that fateful year. The show provides an excellent introduction to the history of the city.

Photographers should be aware that the windows of the observatory have a tinted coating that is often scratched or distorted. Far better photographs can be taken from the observation deck of the Prudential Center, a short walk away, with only 52 storeys.
*John Hancock Observatory, 200 Clarendon Street, Copley Square. Tel: (617) 572–6429. Open: May to October, daily 9am–10pm; November to March Sunday 9am–5pm. Closed: Thanksgiving and Christmas. Admission charge. T station: Copley.*
*Prudential Tower Skywalk, 800 Boylston Street. Tel: (617) 859–0648. Open: daily 10am–10pm. Admission charge. T station: Copley or Prudential.*

John Fitzgerald Kennedy, political idealist;
a hero still in a cynical age

## JOHN F KENNEDY LIBRARY AND MUSEUM

This dramatic building by architect I M Pei is situated on Columbia Point, with sweeping views of the ocean. Although several miles south of downtown Boston, it is nevertheless easily accessible. The Library is the official repository of all of Kennedy's presidential papers and many of his personal belongings. It contains all of his speeches on film and video and also the senatorial papers of Robert F Kennedy. (It is not generally known that the building also houses 95 per cent of the works of Ernest Hemingway.) This is not a library in the traditional sense. The visit starts with a 30-minute film on the life of Kennedy, followed by nine exhibits, many with video displays, relating to JFK, including a re-creation of the Oval Office in the White House. There are two additional exhibits on his brother Robert. Leaving the exhibition you will enter a glass meditation pavilion; beyond is an eight-storey tower where the archives are stored. These are available to the public for research.
*Columbia Point. Tel: (617) 929–4523. Open: daily 9am–5pm. Closed: Thanksgiving, Christmas and New Year's Day. Admission charge. T station: JFK/U Mass (then take the free transfer bus, via the University of Massachusetts, which leaves every 30 minutes from 9am to 5pm).*

From green house to White House: JFK's home

## JOHN F KENNEDY NATIONAL HISTORIC SITE

This grandiose title refers to a small, insignificant house in the suburb of Brookline, restored to its 1917 appearance (when JFK was born there), and most of the contents belonged to the Kennedy family. The house where the Kennedys lived until 1920 is now run by the National Park Service and has exhibits relating to Kennedy and a small bookshop. Of interest only to the most dedicated JFK fans, it is relatively inaccessible, and the JFK Library is of much more interest.
*83 Beals Street, Brookline. Tel: (617) 566–7937. Open: Wednesday to Sunday 10am–4.30pm. Closed: Thanksgiving, Christmas and New Year's Day. Admission charge. T station: Coolridge Corner.*

## KING'S CHAPEL

George Washington, Revolutionary general and first President of the United States, used to attend services at this church, and he attended the musical entertainment that was planned to raise money for the new church building.

The original Anglican church was a wooden building. The present granite building was built around the original church, and the wood was removed piece by piece through the windows. Construction started in 1750, but money ran out before a spire could be added. The oldest pulpit still in use on its original site overlooks an elegant Georgian interior.

Situated next to the church is Boston's oldest cemetery. Issac Johnson, who owned the land, was the first person to be buried here in 1630. He was soon followed by several of the original colonists, including John Winthrop, the first Governor of the colony. The writer Nathaniel Hawthorne used to frequent the cemetery, and it is thought that Elizabeth Pain, who was accused of adultery and buried here in 1705, provided the inspiration for the

King's Chapel, built of local Quincy granite

character of Hester Prynne in his book *The Scarlet Letter.*
*58 Tremont Street. Tel: (617) 523–1749.*
*Open: Monday and Thursday–Saturday 9am–4pm; winter Saturday 9am–4pm.*
*Donation. T station: Government Center.*

### THE KENNEDYS

In 1848 Patrick Kennedy arrived penniless in Boston from Ireland. He made money in saloons and banking and became involved in local politics. His son Joseph married Rose Fitzgerald, the daughter of a long-time mayor of Boston.

Joseph had high political ambitions for his children, and when his eldest son, Joseph Jr, was killed in World War II, John filled his shoes. Kathleen died in a plane crash in 1948 at the age of 28, four years after the death of her husband. After fulfilling his father's ambitions, serving three years as the 35th President of the United States, John was tragically assassinated in 1963. Five years later, his brother Robert suffered the same fate.

The dynasty still hangs on, however, with Edward serving as a United States Senator, and Robert's son Joseph's election to Congress in 1986. The remaining family still gather at the 'Kennedy Compound' at Hyannis Port on Cape Cod.

Lecture in progress in the Ether Dome

## MASSACHUSETTS GENERAL HOSPITAL

A hospital may be the last place you would wish to visit on holiday, but this one has a glorious history. The modern hospital is considered to be one of the best in the United States, and its buildings cover several city blocks. However, it is the original building that is of particular interest.

The Bulfinch Pavilion, designed by Charles Bulfinch in 1816, is hidden in the centre of the modern maze. The best approach is from Cambridge Street to North Grove Street. The Greek Revival building sits incongruously surrounded by the new hospital and, surprisingly, is still in service as an active part of the hospital. The pavilion is topped by an elegant dome that houses what is now called the Ether Room, the hospital's

operating theatre from 1821 to 1867. It was in this room in 1846 that an operation was first performed using an anaesthetic – ether. Within a year, it was being used throughout the world. In 1869 Dr Joseph Lister introduced antiseptics to surgery in this same amphitheatre, and in 1886 the world's first appendectomy was performed, the first procedure involving the opening of the abdominal cavity. The Ether Dome is still in use today, but as a lecture hall. To visit the dome, enter the pavilion and pass through the hospital corridors to the rear elevator, then follow the signs to the dome. If a lecture is in progress, the dome can be entered by a narrow stairway at the rear which leads to the top of the amphitheatre.
*55 Fruit Street. Tel: (617) 726–2000. Open: during normal hospital hours. Free. T station: Charles/MGH.*

## MUSEUM OF FINE ARTS

Boston's premier art gallery is the equal of any gallery in the world, and it is certainly one of America's finest museums. The collections, spread out over two floors, are so exceptional that even a whole day spent here could only give a taste of its treasures. Certain exhibits, however, are important enough to top everyone's list. For a start there is one of the greatest collections of Japanese art in existence. The basis of the collection was gathered by Edward Morse, Sturgis Bigelow and Ernest Fenollosa during their travels in Japan during the 19th century. The collection of Asiatic art as a whole is the largest of any single museum in the world. The collection from Egypt's Old Kingdom, the result of 40 years of excavation in conjunction with Harvard University, is second only to that in the Cairo

Museum. Of particular interest in the fine arts exhibits is a superb collection of Impressionist paintings, including more than 40 by Monet. There are over 150 by Millet, among them his most famous work, *The Sower*, as well as Picasso's *Rape of the Sabine Women*. Twentieth-century painting is perhaps the weakest area, but even so there are impressive canvases by Jackson Pollock, Morris Louis, Robert Motherwell and Georgia O'Keefe. In addition to the wonderful permanent collections, there are regular major touring exhibitions.

*465 Huntington Avenue. Tel: (617) 267–9300. Open: Monday to Friday 10am–4.45pm, Wednesday till 9.45pm, Saturday and Sunday 10am–9.45pm. Closed: major holidays. Admission charge (by voluntary contribution Wednesday 4–9.45pm). Free guided tours Tuesday to Friday 10.30am, 1.30pm, Saturday 11am, 1.30pm. T station: Museum of Fine Arts.*

Impressionism is splendidly represented in the collections of the Museum of Fine Arts

**MUSEUM OF SCIENCE**

This museum is a delight. It extends over two floors of a building located over the Charles River. There are over 140 exhibits, some dating back to 1830 when the museum was founded. Besides the traditional stuffed birds and dioramas, many interactive exhibits encourage the participation of inquisitive young minds. The perennial favourites are the world's largest Van de Graaff generator producing 15-foot bolts of lightning, the talking transparent women and a 20-foot model of T Rex. There is also a 90-foot-long wave machine and a mathematics exhibit that makes the subject interesting to even the most innumerate visitor.

Attached to the museum is the **Charles Hayden Planetarium**, which uses state-of-the-art, multi-image and projection equipment to portray astronomical phenomena or the night skies over Boston. The Mugar Omni Theater shows spectacular films on the 76-foot domed screen.

*Science Park. Tel: (617) 723–2500. Open: daily 9am–5pm; Friday till 9pm. Closed: Thanksgiving and Christmas. Admission charge. T station: Science Park.*

An outsize occupant of the Museum of Science

## NEW ENGLAND AQUARIUM

Appropriately located on Boston's waterfront (see page 52), the aquarium has more than 70 exhibits showing aquatic life from around the world. The centrepiece is a huge three-storey, 187,000-gallon tank, one of the largest in the world, around which spirals a walkway that gives intimate views of over 95 species of fish.

In 1999, the West Wing was completed, providing a 16,500 square foot expansion for a changing exhibit area. The expansion also includes a 200-seat food service area and a larger outdoor exhibit featuring seals and sea otters.

Next door to the aquarium a floating theatre called Discovery presents dolphin and sea-lion shows throughout the day.
*Central Wharf. Tel: (617) 973–5200. Open: Monday to Friday 9am–5pm, Saturday, Sunday and holidays to 6pm.*

Creatures of the deep, quite indifferent to the fascinated scrutiny of aquarium visitors

*Closed: Thanksgiving, Christmas. Admission charge. T station: Aquarium.*

## OLD GRANARY BURYING GROUND

Cemeteries may not seem the most pleasant places to visit, but the Old Granary Burying Ground is a virtual museum of Boston's – and indeed America's – history. Three of the signatories to the Declaration of Independence are buried here, including John Hancock. Here, too, are the graves of the five killed in the Boston Massacre, as well as Paul Revere, the parents of Benjamin Franklin and even Mother Goose! A map at the entrance indicates where the graves are thought to be. Unfortunately, the headstones were rearranged in the 1900s to 'improve' the cemetery's appearance, so it is impossible to know who is actually buried where. The headstones are particularly interesting because of their elaborate 17th-century carvings of skeletons, hour glasses and other suitably macabre motifs.
*Tremont Street, adjacent to Park Street Church. Open: 8am–5pm. T station: Park Street.*

## OLD NORTH CHURCH

Christopher Wren is thought to have inspired the design of this brick church, which is topped by a 175-foot, three-tiered steeple. It is the oldest church in Boston, built in 1723, and is certainly the most famous. On 18 April 1775, Robert Newman placed two lanterns in the belfry to signal to Paul Revere that the British army was advancing towards Concord. Revere's ride to Lexington and Concord to warn the Minutemen that 'the British are coming!' was immortalised in a poem by Longfellow.

Old South Meeting House, where protest meetings denounced British Colonial policies

The church itself has a beautiful, light interior filled with colonial history. Brass plates on the pews indicate their former occupants; look for no 54, which was the pew of the Revere family. On the left side of the vestibule as you leave the church, there is a tablet identifying 12 bricks from Boston, England, that have been set into the wall. They were taken from the prison cell that housed William Brewster and other Pilgrims who were imprisoned when they tried to flee the country in 1607. The bricks were given to the Old North Church by the Mayor of Boston, England, in 1923.

A small museum and gift shop are housed in a former chapel adjacent to the church. On display here is the 'Vinegar Bible', which was a gift from King George II in 1733. It got its name from a printing error which called the Parable of the Vineyard the Parable of the Vinegar.
*193 Salem Street. Tel: (617) 523–6676.*

*Open: daily 9am–6pm. Closed: Thanksgiving and Christmas. T station: Haymarket.*

## OLD SOUTH MEETING HOUSE

This church, which dates from 1729, is the second oldest in the city, and within its walls the Boston Tea Party was planned. Over 5,000 people gathered here in December of 1773 to protest against the despised tea tax imposed by the British (see pages 46 and 50). Audio tours of the church are available, and there are exhibits relating to many of the Meeting Houses's early congregation members, including black poet Phillis Wheatley, patriot Samuel Adams and Elizabeth Vergoose – the original Mother Goose.
*310 Washington Street. Tel: (617) 482–6439. Open: November to March, 10am–4pm; April to October, 9.30am–5pm. Entrance charge. T station: State.*

Benjamin Franklin, baptised in the original Meeting House in 1706, greets visitors

A 931-pound bronze bell cast by Revere, considered the best bell-maker of his time

## OLD STATE HOUSE

Boston's oldest public building (see page 47), dating back to 1713, is now incongruously surrounded by modern commercial buildings. Until the Revolution this was the colonial headquarters of the British Government. The British symbols of the lion and unicorn on the gables of the building are copies; the originals were burned on 4 July 1776, when the colonies declared independence. Inside is a museum of Boston's maritime history. Surprisingly for such a historic monument, the T station is inside the building.

Directly across State Street is the National Park Visitor Center (tel: 617 242–5642), which is not only a valuable source of information but is also the starting point for ranger-led tours of the city. The center also has good public toilets – a rarity in Boston.

*206 Washington Street. Tel: (617) 720–3290. Open: daily 9am–5pm. Closed: major holidays. Admission charge. T station: State.*

## PAUL REVERE HOUSE

This simple clapboard house is the last remaining 17th-century structure in Boston. Silversmith, engraver, printer and patriot Paul Revere lived here from 1770 to 1800, and a few of the family's original furnishings remain. The Revere House is a major stop on the tourist circuit, and long queues often form to visit this tiny dwelling.

*19 North Square. Tel: (617) 523–2338. Open: daily 9.30am–5.15pm; winter 9.30am–4.15pm. Closed: Monday from January to March. Admission charge. T station: Haymarket.*

## PAUL REVERE MALL

Set in the heart of Boston's North End, this tree-lined park has become a meeting place for the local Italian community. On a summer's afternoon, old men come out to gossip and enjoy a game of cards or checkers (draughts). The Mall, or Prado as the locals call it, is dominated at one end by a famous statue of Paul Revere on horseback and at the other by the Old North Church. *No convenient T station.*

## PUBLIC GARDEN

The Public Garden is a continuation of the Boston Common, but the difference is immediately obvious. The Public Garden was the first botanical garden in the country and is perfectly landscaped and manicured, with a weeping willow-fringed central lagoon. Boston's famous 'swan boats' have been a familiar sight on the lagoon every summer since 1877 when they were first introduced; they operate from April to September 10am–5pm (small charge). The garden also has a diverse collection of statuary depicting, among others, George Washington on horseback and Mrs Mallard and her eight ducklings, a larger-than-life family much loved by children. In asking for directions to the garden, be sure to specify the *Public* Garden (*Boston Garden*, a well-known sports arena, was replaced by the FleetCenter in 1996). *T station: Arlington.*

## STATE HOUSE

The golden-domed classical building crowning Beacon Hill was described by Oliver Wendell Holmes as 'the hub of the solar system'. It was designed by the great Boston architect Charles Bulfinch, and the cornerstones were laid by Paul Revere and Sam Adams in 1795. The interior is magnificent. The Hall of Flags, directly under the dome, was built to house a collection of Civil War battle flags; murals depicting Revere's ride and the Boston Tea Party decorate the Senate Staircase Hall, and floors throughout the building are made of 24 kinds of marble. In the House Chamber hangs a famous wooden fish, the 'Sacred Cod' of Massachusetts, which has been symbolising the importance of the fishing industry since 1784. In the basement archives and museum are copies of the Mayflower Compact, the State Charter granted by Charles I, and many other treasured historic documents. Entrance into the State House is via a side door. Only US Presidents, or State Governors leaving the House for the last time, use the main doors (see page 46).
*Beacon Street. Tel: (617) 727–3676. Open: Monday to Friday 9am–5pm. Tours: every 30 minutes, 10am–4pm. Closed: state holidays. T station: Park Street.*

The dignified façade of the State House, whose dome was painted black in World War II

## MARITIME HISTORY

From the time the Pilgrims landed on Cape Cod, New England has had an intimate relationship with the sea. Whaling was the major industry during the 18th century, reaching its peak between 1820 and 1860 with large fleets in New Bedford and Nantucket.

Maritime commerce was always an important industry, from the infamous 'Triangle Trade' (molasses for rum for slaves) to the 'China Trade' out of the ports of Salem, Boston and Providence.

Today maritime activity is mainly the preserve of leisure craft and many thousands of recreational sailors ply the waters once ruled by the Captain Ahabs of the past.

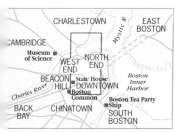

# The Freedom Trail

This is the perfect introduction to Colonial and Revolutionary Boston. Collect a free leaflet and follow the red line for 3 miles through the historic downtown area. *The walk merits a whole day, but can be completed in 3 hours.*

*Start at the Park Street T station. An information booth offers free maps and brochures about the trail.*

### 1 STATE HOUSE
Cross the Boston Common to the State House (see page 45).
*Return along Park Street, turning left at the church.*

### 2 OLD GRANARY BURYING GROUND

The cemetery is on the left (see page 42).
*Continue to School Street.*

### 3 KING'S CHAPEL AND BURYING GROUND
These are located on the right corner (see page 39). Continue down School Street. In front of the Old City Hall is a statue of Benjamin Franklin.
*Continue to the end of the street.*

### 4 GLOBE CORNER BOOKSTORE
The Globe Corner Bookstore (formerly the Old Corner Bookstore) is on the left corner (see page 36).
*Turn right into Washington Street.*

### 5 OLD SOUTH MEETING HOUSE
The Meeting House is on the left (see pages 43 and 50). In front of the building is an excellent flower stand.
*Return along Washington Street and turn right into State Street.*

The red line linking historic sites since 1951

## 6 OLD STATE HOUSE

This is opposite the National Park Visitor Center, which has an excellent bookstore and toilets (see page 44).

*Continue right on State Street, past the Boston Massacre site. Turn left into Congress Street.*

## 7 FANEUIL HALL AND QUINCY MARKET

Faneuil Hall is on the right (see page 35). Behind it is Quincy Market (a perfect lunch stop).

*From Faneuil Hall turn right into Union Street. Pass the Union Oyster House, on the right; the new civic complex is near by. Turn right into Hanover Street and cross Blackstone Street, with its weekly outdoor market. Notice the brass fruit, vegetables and rubbish set into the pavement. Pass under the freeway, turn right into Cross Street, turn first left and continue to Parmenter Street. Turn right, then left into North Street.*

## 8 PAUL REVERE HOUSE

This is on the left (see page 44). Continue up North Street, turn left into Prince Street, then right into Hanover Street. St Stephen's is the only church designed by Charles Bulfinch that remains in Boston.

*Cross Hanover Street and walk to the end of Paul Revere Mall (see page 44).*

## 9 OLD NORTH CHURCH

The church is straight in front of you (see page 42). Leaving it, walk up Hull Street (excellent views from the top).

## 10 COPP'S HILL BURYING GROUND

The cemetery gates are on the right (see page 35).

*You can finish here and visit Charlestown*

Footsore Freedom Trailers can rest in the Mall and admire an equestrian Paul Revere

*separately, or continue down Hull Street, then left into Commercial Street and right across the Charlestown Bridge, to the Puritans' first point of settlement, now called City Square. Continue along Water Street, where Bunker Hill Pavilion has a good audio-visual programme.*

## 11 USS *CONSTITUTION*

The *Constitution* is in Charlestown Navy Yard (see pages 30–1). Adjacent is the Constitution Museum.

*From this point, the red line is often obliterated, so ask for precise directions at the museum.*

## 12 BUNKER HILL MONUMENT

Sitting atop Breed's Hill, the monument offers good views over the navy yard (see page 30). The trail ends here.

*To return, walk down Lexington Street for a bus or taxi (no T service).*

# The Black Heritage Trail

This trail celebrates the history of Boston's black community between 1800 and 1900, when they settled in this part of Beacon Hill (see pages 26–7). It passes all the most interesting houses in the area and gives a glimpse of Victorian Boston. See map on pages 24–5 for route. *The walk takes about 2 hours, including stops.*

*From Park Street T station, cross the Boston Common towards the State House.*

## 1 SHAW MEMORIAL

Located opposite the State House in Beacon Street, this impressive bas-relief by Augustus Saint-Gauden honours the

service of African-Americans in the Civil War. The first black regiment in the North was recruited in Massachusetts and led by Shaw, a young white officer from Boston who volunteered for the post.
*Walk down Beacon Street, turn right into Joy Street and left into Pinckney Street.*

## 2 PHILLIPS SCHOOL

This institution, at the corner of Anderson Street, was one of the first Boston public schools to have an inter-racial student body.
*Continue on Pinckney Street to number 86.*

## 3 JOHN J SMITH HOUSE

Smith was a distinguished black statesman who moved to Boston in 1848. A barber's shop owned by him was a centre of black abolitionist activity and a meeting place for runaway slaves.
*Continue down Pinckney Street, turn left into West Cedar Street and right into Mount Vernon Street. Walk down to Charles Street.*

## 4 CHARLES STREET MEETING HOUSE

The Meeting House remained in use as a church until 1939, when it was the last black institution to leave Beacon Hill.
*Continue down Charles Street to Revere Street, turn right, then left into West Cedar Street and right into Phillips Street.*

## 5 LEWIS AND HARRIET HAYDEN HOUSE

This house, at No 66, was a stop on the 'underground railroad' after the Fugitive Slave Law was passed in 1850. Lewis Hayden was eventually elected to the

The Shaw Memorial, depicting the farewell march of the 54th Regiment down Beacon Street

State Legislature, and Harriet Hayden established a scholarship fund for black students at Harvard Medical School.
*Continue up Phillips Street to the corner of Irving Street.*

## 6 COBURN'S GAMING HOUSE

In 1844 John P Coburn founded this establishment as a private club that served as 'the resort of the upper ten who had acquired a taste for gambling'.
*Turn left down to Cambridge Street. Turn right and right again into Joy Street, then right again into Smith Court.*

## 7 AFRICAN MEETING HOUSE

On the left at the end of Smith Court is the completely renovated African Meeting House, the oldest black church building (1806) still standing in America. The ground floor houses a small museum.

## 8 SMITH COURT RESIDENCES

These are directly opposite the Meeting House, and they are typical of the homes occupied by black Bostonians throughout the 19th century.
*Return to the corner of Joy Street.*

## 9 ABEL SMITH SCHOOL

Now housing the Museum of Afro-American History, this school was built in 1834 to educate black grammar school students.
*Continue up Joy Street to 5 Pinckney Street.*

## 10 GEORGE MIDDLETON HOUSE

Middleton, a colonel in the Revolution, commanded an all-black company. His is the oldest home built by a black person on Beacon Hill.
*This is the end of the trail. It is only a short walk back to Beacon Street and the Boston Common.*

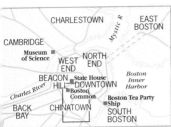

# The Women's Heritage Trail

This trail, passing through Chinatown and the theatre district, highlights buildings where notable women have either lived or worked.

See map on pages 24–5 for route. *The walk can easily be completed in 90 minutes.*

*Start in Washington Street.*

### 1 OLD SOUTH MEETING HOUSE

Displays feature the work of freed slave and poet Phillis Wheatley (an early member of the congregation) and that of historic preservationist Mary Hemenway (see pages 43 and 46). *Leave the Meeting House, turn left and then left again into Milk Street.*

### 2 MILK STREET

Writer Franklin Mecom lived at 15–17 Milk Street in the 18th century.
*Return to Washington Street and continue left through the downtown shopping area to West Street. Turn right.*

### 3 WEST STREET

In the mid-19th century No 13 was the bookshop of Elizabeth Peabody, who introduced kindergartens to New England.
*Return to Washington Street, turn right past the Opera Company of Boston founded by Sarah Caldwell, left into Avenue de Lafayette and right into Chauncy Street, leading to Harrison Avenue.*

### 4 HARRISON STREET

At Nos 2–8, Julia O'Conner led a successful strike of 8,000 women telephone operators in 1919, paralysing

Old South Meeting House

the whole of New England for a week.
*Continue down Harrison Avenue to Beach Street, turn left, then right into Tyler Street.*

## 5 TYLER STREET

In 1761 the slave ship *Phillis* landed at Avery Wharf; among its human cargo was a child who became known as Phillis Wheatley, the first black female poet to be published in America. At 2 Tyler Street is the Chinese Women's Association, founded in 1942 in response to Madame Chiang Kai Shek's appeal for China relief. Number 76 was the home of the Lebanese-Syrian Ladies Aid Society, founded in 1917 to raise money for new arrivals and to provide relief to the Near East. Number 79 belongs to the Maryknoll Sisters of St Dominic, known for their service in China prior to the Communist takeover. They now serve worldwide, particularly in Latin America. Quincy School at number 90 opened in 1847 and, for the first time, American teachers had their own classrooms, and pupils their own desks. Although this was a boys' school, the teachers were women.
*Continue to the end of Tyler Street and turn right into Oak Street.*

## 6 OAK STREET

The mural at 34 Oak Street symbolises Asian-American women in the garment industry.
*Continue along Oak Street to Tremont Street and turn right.*

## 7 CHINESE CULTURAL INSTITUTE

The art gallery at 276 Tremont Street was founded in 1980 by Doris C J Chu to promote racial harmony through cultural understanding. Plaques along Tremont Street theatre walls name famous actresses who have played there.
*Turn left into Stuart Street and walk through Transportation Building to Boylston Place.*

## 8 BOYLSTON PLACE

Number 5 is where the Boston Women's Trade Union League was based during the Great Depression.
*Turn left into Boylston Street to Park Square.*

## 9 PARK SQUARE

From her office here, Pauline Hopkins edited *The Colored American* from 1900 to 1904.
*Return along Boylston Street to Tremont Street and turn left towards Boston Common.*

## 10 TREMONT STREET

Number 174 was the Boston School of Cooking, the first professional school in Boston for women cooks. Fanny Farmer published her famous cookbook from here in 1896; it sold over 3 million copies.
*Continue to Park Street T station.*

Portrait of Mary Hemenway at the Old South Meeting House

CHARLESTOWN
EAST BOSTON
Mystic R
CAMBRIDGE
Museum of Science
NORTH END
WEST END
BEACON HILL
State House
DOWNTOWN
Boston Common
Boston
Boston Inner Harbor
Charles River
CHINATOWN
BACK BAY
Boston Tea Party Ship
SOUTH BOSTON

# The Boston Waterfront

Since the foundation of Boston, the waterfront has changed out of all recognition. Shipping is now reduced to ferries, sightseeing boats and pleasure craft; landfill has created a new, modern waterfront with good restaurants where property is among the most expensive in the city. This walk illustrates some of the changes that have evolved over the centuries. See map on pages 24–5 for route. *Allow 1½ hours.*

*Start at the Old State House (State Street T station). Cross Congress Street and walk down State Street towards the water. Look for the Cunard sign at 126 State Street, a reminder of days when the big ships came to Boston. Continue down to India Street.*

## 1 CUSTOM HOUSE

This became the tallest building in Boston in 1915 when a 30-storey clock tower was added to the original Greek Revival building. In late 1996 it opened as a timeshare owned by Marriot Vacation Club. When open, the 25th-floor observation deck gives excellent views of the harbour and the financial district.

*Continue across Atlantic Avenue.*

## 2 CHRISTOPHER COLUMBUS PARK

Opened in 1976, this park is ideal for a picnic and for watching the harbour traffic and planes taking off from Logan Airport across the water. For picnic supplies, Quincy Market is only five minutes away.

## 3 LONG WHARF

This is Boston's oldest wharf, dating back to 1710, and before landfill it extended for half a mile up State Street, almost to the Old State House. In its day it was the major centre of activity for sea-going voyages and delivery of cargo. Views from the end of the wharf are as sweeping as ever.

## 4 NEW ENGLAND AQUARIUM

Just one wharf over from Long Wharf, the aquarium continues to be one of Boston's favourite attractions (see page 42). Sit for a while and watch the harbour seals in their outdoor pool by the entrance.

*Continue south along the waterfront.*

## 5 ROWES WHARF

The 1987 Rowes Wharf complex, with its huge six-storey arch, houses a luxury

Christopher Columbus Park

hotel, apartments, offices and shops. The water-shuttle to Logan Airport leaves from here, and it is well worth taking the 7-minute trip just to experience its picturesque approach to the city.

*Continue alongside Atlantic Avenue, turn left into Northern Avenue and cross the bridge. Turn right into Sleeper Street.*

## 6 COMPUTER MUSEUM

Housed in an old leather and wool warehouse, the Computer Museum has an external glass lift giving views of the Fort Point Channel (see page 35).

## 7 CHILDREN'S MUSEUM

Although it shares the same building as the Computer Museum, the Children's Museum can be identified by a 40-foot milk bottle, actually a fast-food stand (see page 31).

*Cross Congress Street Bridge.*

## 8 BOSTON TEA PARTY SHIP

Half-way across the bridge on the right is the Boston Tea Party Ship. The original location has long since vanished to landfill, but the ship is a full-scale working replica with a small, lively museum (see page 29).

*Continue across the bridge and turn left into Dorchester Avenue, then right into Summer Street. Continue to Atlantic Avenue.*

## 9 SOUTH STATION

This was the biggest railway station in the world when it was completed in 1900. Most of the original granite station has been demolished, but the impressive entrance remains. The present building is a careful restoration. The cavernous terminal is bustling with cafés, vendors and shops.

*The walk ends here, and there is a T station at South Station.*

# Architecture

New England is a living museum of the history of American architecture, from the earliest colonial styles to contemporary modernists. In Boston the name Charles Bulfinch occurs with predictable regularity. He was New England's most prolific architect during the early 1800s, designing both residential and civic buildings, culminating in the Capitol Building in Washington DC. The architecture of the region falls into six periods.

## Early Colonial

The first houses built in New England were simple, wood-shingled cottages with classical symmetry, usually incorporating medieval design elements such as an overhanging second storey and a massive central chimney. Often a 'lean-to' was added, resulting in the New England 'saltbox' that can still be seen all over Cape Cod.

## Georgian

By the end of the 1700s, greater prosperity created a demand for larger, more spacious houses, and the elegant Georgian architecture of England was introduced first to Boston, as early as 1686, and much later elsewhere in New

Cottages at Oak Bluffs, Martha's Vineyard, with beautifully executed detailing

England. These symmetric brick or wooden buildings, with hipped roofs and careful, stripped detail, were built to the exact standards of proportion developed during the Italian Renaissance. Earlier casement windows lost favour and were replaced by sash windows with smaller rectangular panes.

## Federal

This post-Revolutionary extension of the Georgian style was more delicate, with many design features inspired by England's Adam brothers. A unique feature of this New England architecture was the balustrade surrounding the roof on houses built near the sea. This 'widow's walk' gave seafarers' wives a high vantage point from which to look out for their husbands' boats.

## Greek Revival

Rounded arches, shallow domes and low pitched pediments are all features of this style that was based on the temples of ancient Greece. It was popular in the southern part of New England for civic and commercial buildings; Boston's Quincy Market is a good example.

## Victorian

The Victorians developed many different schools of architecture. One of the most nationally influential, known as Richardson Romanesque, used massive stonework and powerful arches. The style lives on in libraries and city halls throughout the nation. Gothic Revival also reared its head during this period, producing houses covered in the ornate trim that was now so easily made with machinery. Stained glass was also widely used, as were polychrome bands of tile and brickwork. The Beaux Arts movement brought the new Renaissance

Boston's South End: a harmonious contrast of curves and angles in brownstone houses

to New England, and the strong French influence can be seen in many mansions in Newport, Rhode Island.

## Contemporary

New England boasts a *Who's Who* of contemporary architecture. The great Bauhaus architect Walter Gropius – one of the prime figures in modern architecture combining function with simplicity – left Germany in 1937 and moved to Harvard as Director of the School of Architecture. Since then virtually every major architect has designed at least one New England building. I M Pei's work seems to be everywhere, and there are several buildings in the Boston and Cambridge areas by Eero Saarinen, Philip Johnson, Louis Kahn and James Stirling.

# Cambridge

*A*lthough their histories have long been intertwined, Cambridge is a separate city from Boston. Green lawns, towering trees, red-brick quadrangles, the Charles River with people sculling along its sweeping curve – all are set off by an invigorating 20th-century atmosphere, young, bustling and trendy.

Newtowne, as it was first called, was established in 1630 and became the first capital of the Massachusetts Bay Colony. In 1636 a college was founded – the first in America – for the purpose of training young men for the ministry (see page 64). That same year the town was renamed Cambridge, after the town in England where many of the Puritans had completed their studies.

In 1639 the first printing press in the New World was established in Cambridge, and the document *The Oath of the Free Man* became the very first American publication.

In 1916 the prestigious Massachusetts Institute of Technology (MIT) left Boston and crossed the river; together with Harvard University it forms one of the premier seats of learning in the world. Today Cambridge exudes an academic atmosphere – which is not surprising, since almost half of its 96,000 population is involved in education and the universities.

The heart of Cambridge is Harvard

## CAMBRIDGE

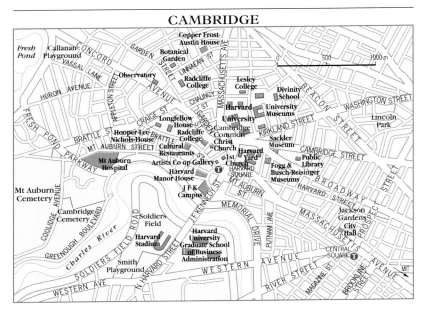

Christ Church, designed by Peter Harrison, architect of King's Chapel, Boston

Square (actually a triangle). In the centre of the square is the landmark Out of Town News, with newspapers and magazines from every corner of the globe.

Most of the major sites are within easy walking distance of the Square.

### BRATTLE STREET

The wealthy Loyalist Tories of the 18th century built grand houses along the western end of Brattle Street, giving it the name Tory Row. Fine examples are the Ruggles Fayerweather House at 175 and the Hooper-Lee-Nichols House at 159.

### CHRIST CHURCH

Built in 1760, this simple grey and white building – the oldest church in Cambridge – sits on the edge of Cambridge Common. A brass plaque marks the pew where George Washington and his wife worshipped on New Year's Eve in 1775. On the wall of the vestibule is a bullet hole reputedly from a British rifle as the Redcoats marched on to Lexington. Under an elm tree on the Common, a

plaque marks the spot where General Washington took command of the Continental Army in 1775. Close by are three British cannons that were abandoned at Fort Independence. *Garden Street. Tel: (617) 876–0200. Open: daily 9am–5pm. Free.*

Interior of Longfellow's House, Brattle Street

# Harvard University

*T*he whole of Cambridge revolves around this venerable institution. The university has over 400 buildings spread over 380 acres of land. There are seven museums and more than a hundred libraries.

## HARVARD YARD

The Yard is the oldest part of the campus. Walk across from Harvard Square and enter the first quadrangle. On the western side of the Yard is Massachusetts Hall; built in 1720, it is the oldest Harvard building still standing.

Opposite is the famous statue of John Harvard by Daniel Chester French. The inscription 'John Harvard, Founder 1638' has earned the statue its nickname, 'The Statue of Three Lies': French used a student, not Harvard himself, as a model for the statue; John Harvard was not the founder but a benefactor; and the college was founded two years earlier, in 1636.

The Yard is a series of interconnected squares, each surrounded by academic buildings dating from the early 1700s to the present day. These green oases offer a tranquil alternative to the bustle of Harvard Square.

## ARTHUR M SACKLER MUSEUM

British architect James Stirling designed this post-modern building, which was completed in 1986. It houses a remarkable collection of ancient Asian and Islamic art, including some of the world's finest Chinese jade. There is also a particularly good collection of

Harvard's grounds were once used as cattle yards, hence the term Harvard Yard

Japanese woodblock prints. The Harvard University art museum shop is located here, and special exhibitions are also featured throughout the year.
*485 Broadway. Tel: (617) 495–9400. Open: Monday to Saturday 10am–6pm, Sunday 1pm–5pm. Free tours daily at 1pm. Admission charge (includes Fogg and Busch-Reisinger Museums). Free Wednesday and Saturday from 10am–noon.*

## BUSCH-REISINGER MUSEUM

Entered through the Fogg, this museum includes a unique collection of 20th-century German art, particularly the Expressionist movement. Other periods of German and some Eastern European art are also represented, along with decorative arts, architectural drawings and sculpture.
*32 Quincy Street. Tel: (617) 495–9400. Open: Monday to Saturday 10am–5pm, Sunday from 1pm. Admission charge (includes Fogg and Sackler Museums). Free Saturday from 10am–noon.*

## FOGG ART MUSEUM

This art gallery was founded in 1891 and is the oldest of the Harvard art museums. The galleries are on two levels surrounding an Italian Renaissance courtyard and contain a comprehensive collection of Western art. Particularly notable are the Impressionist paintings, British pre-Raphaelite works and Italian Renaissance paintings. Concerts are often held in the central courtyard.

A gallery of decorative arts has displays of furniture, clocks, china, etc from Harvard's vast collection. Included here is the President's Chair, brought to Harvard in the mid-1700s by the Reverend Edward Holyoke and used during commencement ceremonies by every Harvard president since then.

Well-displayed period furnishings complement the Fogg's superb paintings and sculpture

*32 Quincy Street. Tel: (617) 495–9400. Open: as Busch-Reisinger Museum. Free tours daily at 11am, 2pm. Admission charge (includes Busch-Reisinger and Sackler Museums). Free Wednesday and Saturday from 10am–noon.*

## MUSEUMS OF NATURAL HISTORY

Four distinct museums share the same building in Oxford Street (see box on page 60 for practical details). As they are in the middle of the University complex, parking is next to impossible. However, there are parking meters exclusively for museum visitors just off Oxford Street, and there is usually space available.

### Botanical Museum

If there is only time to visit one museum in this fascinating complex, then it has to be the Botanical Museum. The centrepiece here is the remarkable 'Garden in Glass'. Between 1887 and 1936 over 840 species of plants and flowers were made entirely from glass by brothers Leopold and Rudolf Blaska. Sadly, sonic booms shattered some of the models; the 700 or so that survived are displayed in glass cases, in an appropriately Victorian atmosphere.

Memorial Church, with Bulfinch-style steeple

the 25,000-year-old Harvard mastodon and the coelacanth (the fish thought to have been extinct for 70 million years but recently rediscovered) are also on display.

### Peabody Museum of Archeology and Ethnology
Founded in 1866, this is the oldest cultural museum in North America. It boasts one of the most important collections of American Indian culture in the world – the result of many Harvard-sponsored expeditions to North, Central and South America – and some items were brought back by the Lewis and Clark Expedition of 1804–6. The Mayan collection is particularly strong. Throughout the museum dioramas represent different tribal habitats.

### Geological and Mineralogical Museum
This comprehensive collection of rocks, minerals and crystals has a distinctly Victorian feel to it. The most interesting specimens are the giant gypsum crystals from Mexico and a 3,040-carat topaz.

### Museum of Comparative Zoology
This traditional collection of fossils, bones and stuffed animals has a number of highlights. The Thayer Hall displays every species of bird that breeds north of Mexico. There is the world's oldest egg, laid 225 million years ago. Skeletons of

### MEMORIAL CHURCH
The church directly opposite the Widener Library was built as a memorial to the men of Harvard who died in World War I. It contains one of the great baroque organs of America built by C B Fisk.

### WIDENER MEMORIAL LIBRARY
The Widener Memorial Library impressively overlooks the second quadrangle of the Yard. This modern, Corinthian-colonnaded building, dating back only to 1913, is the third-largest library in the whole of North America, with countless manuscripts and first editions. It also houses the only remaining volume from John Harvard's collection. In 1764 a massive fire destroyed the 5,000-volume library which contained his complete collection. One single volume had been borrowed by a student the night before the fire. When he returned the book, according to legend, the president profusely thanked· the student – and then expelled him for

---

**MUSEUMS OF NATURAL HISTORY**
24 Oxford Street. Tel: (617) 495–2326 (Botanical); (617) 495–4758 (Mineralogical); (617) 495–2463 (Zoology); (617) 495–2248 (Peabody). Open: Monday to Saturday 9am–4.30pm, Sunday 1–4.30pm. Admission charge. Free Saturday 9–11am.

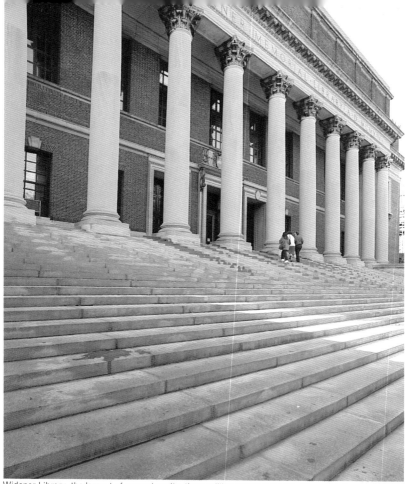

Widener Library, the largest of any university: three million volumes on 50 miles of shelves

taking the book without permission!

The library was named after Harry Elkins Widener, a Harvard alumnus of 1907, whose parents donated funds to complete the building in 1915. Young Harry went down with the *Titanic* because, the story goes, he returned to his cabin to rescue a first edition of Francis Bacon's essays.

In the Harry Elkins Widener Memorial Room there is a display of his collection, which includes one of the remaining 50 Gutenburg Bibles and a first folio of Shakespeare dating back to 1623. There are also dioramas showing Cambridge in 1667, 1775 and 1936 and murals by John Singer Sargent in the stair hall.

*Harvard Yard. Tel: (617) 495–4166.*
*Open: Monday to Friday 9am–10pm,*
*Saturday 9am–5pm, Sunday noon–5pm*
*in term time. T station: Harvard.*

Longfellow House: this clapboard building was abandoned by its Loyalist owner in 1774

## LONGFELLOW NATIONAL HISTORIC SITE

This magnificent Georgian dwelling, with sunny yellow clapboarding, shutters and grand entrance, was used by George Washington as his headquarters during the siege of Boston in 1775–6. It is now operated by the National Park Service.

Henry Wadsworth Longfellow, who taught at Harvard, rented a room here in 1837, and when he married wealthy heiress Fanny Appleton, his father-in-law gave them the house as a wedding gift. Theirs was a happy marriage, and they had six children, but Fanny died tragically after 18 years when her hooped skirt caught fire – she was melting sealing wax to preserve locks of their children's hair. Longfellow, bearing dreadful facial scars from his attempts to save his wife, continued to live in the house for a further 27 years. He wrote many of his best-known poems here, including *Paul Revere's Ride*, *The Song of Hiawatha* and *Evangaline*, and visitors included Dickens, Twain, Emerson, Hawthorne and Wilde.

The furnishings are virtually as they were in Longfellow's time, and visitors can see his study, many of his personal possessions and hundreds of books from his library, as well as the Steinway piano, around which he enjoyed singing German *Leider*.

*105 Brattle Street. Tel: (617) 876–4491. Open: Wednesday to Friday noon–4.30pm, Saturday and Sunday 10am–4.30pm, summer Wednesday to Sunday 10am–4.30pm. Closed: Christmas, Thanksgiving and New Year's Day. Admission charge.*

## MASSACHUSETTS INSTITUTE OF TECHNOLOGY (MIT)

Opposite Harvard – in its architecture and atmosphere as well as geographically – MIT has been representing the best education in engineering and technology since 1861. Set on the banks of the Charles River, the modern campus and its geometrical buildings, designed by the likes of Eero Saarinen and I M Pei, form a suitable reflection of the Institute's high-tech emphasis.

The MIT Museum is actually a group of four museums, all of which complement the more traditional approach of the Harvard museums.

The **Main Exhibition Center** houses a collection of architectural plans, photographs, scientific instruments and other artefacts relating to the Institute. There are interactive plasma globes, mathematical sculptures, holography exhibits, demonstrations of photo-micrography and many other fascinating examples of the frontiers of science.

The **Compton Gallery** has exhibits showing the interaction between art and science, while the **Hart Nautical Galleries** contain a renowned collection of ship models, plans, marine art and engine models.

In **Strobe Alley** there is an exhibition of the work and equipment of scientist and photographer Harold Edgerton, an MIT faculty member who was a pioneer in the use of stroboscopic lighting.

The **List Visual Arts Center**, also on the MIT campus, has three galleries displaying the most interesting and controversial art in a variety of media.

## RADCLIFFE COLLEGE

Radcliffe was founded in 1879 to permit Harvard professors to teach women, who were not allowed admission to Harvard as students. Its name honours Lady Anne Radcliffe Mowlson, a 17th-century British benefactor of Harvard who established that college's first scholarship. Longfellow's daughter, Alice, was instrumental in the college's foundation.

Radcliffe remained a sister institution to Harvard until 1975, when the administrations were merged and equal admission standards were adopted for both men and women.

Entering the Radcliffe campus off Brattle Street, visitors discover graceful old school buildings surrounding a delightful landscaped quadrangle with a perfect lawn.

Of all the buildings at Radcliffe, the most important is the **Schlesinger Library**, which houses the largest and most comprehensive collection of women's literature in the country. The library contains the archives of many notable women, including suffragists Susan B Anthony and Julia Ward Howe.

---

**MIT**

**Main Exhibition Center**, 265 Massachusetts Avenue. Tel: (617) 253–4444. Open: Tuesday to Friday 9am–5pm, Saturday and Sunday 1–5pm. Admission charge.
**Compton Gallery**, **Hart Nautical Galleries** and **Strobe Alley**, 77 Massachusetts Avenue. Tel: (617) 253–4444. Open: daily 9am–8pm; **Compton Gallery** Monday to Friday 9am–5pm. Free. T station: Central.
**List Visual Arts Center**, 20 Ames Street. Tel: (617) 253–4680. Open: Tuesday to Thursday, Saturday and Sunday noon–6pm, Friday noon–8pm. Free. T station: Kendall.

# ALMA MATERS

The Puritans realised that higher education was an essential foundation on which to build their ideal society. As a consequence, New England has a greater concentration of first-class universities than any part of the country. The traditional academic atmosphere of these venerable institutions can be traced directly back to the Oxford or Cambridge roots of their founders.

Newtowne College was founded in 1636 primarily to train young men for the Puritan clergy. The name was changed to Harvard College two years later, after John Harvard died and bequeathed his library of 400 books and half his fortune to the college.

The Collegiate School of Saybrook, founded by Harvard graduates in 1701, moved to New Haven, Connecticut, in 1716. Two years later it was renamed Yale after its benefactor, Elihu Yale.

In 1755 the Reverend Eleazar Wheelock founded Moore's Indian Charity School in Hanover, New Hampshire. The name was changed to Dartmouth College in 1769. Tuition is still free to members of the Six Nations Confederation.

In 1764 Nicholas Brown, a prominent Rhode Island merchant whose family had made their fortune in the China trade, founded Rhode Island College as a Baptist school. In 1804 the name was changed to Brown University.

Thus the foundation of Ivy League education

Ivy-covered Yale (above), with Trumbull College's arch (right)

was established. ('Ivy League' refers to the classical ivy-covered buildings that formed the core of each of these Eastern US colleges.)

In complete contrast are the many new concrete-and-glass technological universities that have mushroomed in the last century, building on the firm traditional scholastic base already in place. Heading the list – though hardly new, dating from 1861 – is the Massachusetts Institute of Technology (MIT), with many other colleges close behind.

Altogether there are 269 colleges and universities, 7.5 per cent of the

Harvard's Widener Library (top); the ready-to-wear preppie look (above left); MIT's Great Court and MacLaruin Building (above)

total for the whole United States. In the Greater Boston area alone there are 65 such institutions.

# North of Boston

*A*lthough it takes less than an hour to drive from Boston to the New Hampshire border, that short distance contains more history, culture and scenery than many of the other 49 states. Two of the most significant towns in American history lie just a brief journey from the capital.

## CONCORD

To most Americans Concord and Lexington (see pages 68–9) are inextricably linked. Although close together geographically and historically, Concord has both greater charm and greater vitality than Lexington, and it has a much broader range of sites to visit.

On 19 April 1775, after the confrontation at Lexington, the British marched on to Concord, where 400 Minutemen waited near the Old North Bridge. They forced the British into a retreat to Boston in what was the first serious battle of the American Revolution.

The **Concord Museum** contains 15 period rooms and galleries that present local history through decorative arts and

The Old Manse: Emerson's grandfather watched the battle of North Bridge from here

domestic artefacts. Displays include the contents of Emerson's study, the simple furniture from Thoreau's Walden Pond cabin, and one of the lanterns that signalled to Paul Revere.
*200 Lexington Road. Tel: (508) 369–9609. Open: January to March, Monday to Saturday 11am–4pm, Sunday from 1pm; April to December, Monday to Saturday 9am–5pm, Sunday from noon. Admission charge.*

**Minute Man National Historical Park** has a visitor centre showing films and exhibits relating to the battle. Walk down to the Old North Bridge (actually a modern replica) and the Daniel Chester French statue of a Minuteman, made from melted 1776 cannon.
*Start at Battle Road Visitor Center, off Route 2A on Airport Road. Tel: (508) 369–6993. Open: daily 8.30am–5pm; extended summer hours.*

**Literary Concord**
A few minutes' walk from the Old North Bridge is the **Old Manse**. Ralph Waldo Emerson lived here for a period, then the house was occupied by Nathaniel Hawthorne for two years while he was writing *Mosses from an Old Manse*. The house is full of Hawthorne and Emerson memorabilia and original furniture.
*Monument Street. Tel: (508) 369–3909.*

Emerson moved to the **Ralph Waldo Emerson House**, where he lived from 1835 to 1882. The restored

Thoreau's Walden Pond: 'I went to the woods...to front only the essential facts of life.'

house is furnished as it was during his time. _28 Cambridge Turnpike. Tel: (508) 369–2236._

Hawthorne, who wrote _The House of Seven Gables_ and _The Scarlet Letter_, lived for some time at **The Wayside** after buying it from the Alcott family. _455 Lexington Road. Tel: (508) 369–6975._

The Alcotts moved on to **Orchard House** and lived here for almost 20 years. Louisa May wrote both _Little Women_ and _Little Men_ at this house. _399 Lexington Road. Tel: (508) 369–4118._

The other major figure in the Concord Group, as they called themselves, was Henry David Thoreau, whose _Walden_ has become an American classic on environmentalism. For two years he lived a life of contemplation and reflection on nature in a cabin by Walden Pond. The **Thoreau Lyceum**, headquarters of the Thoreau Society, has a replica of that cabin and an extensive library and collection of memorabilia. _156 Belknap Street. Tel: (508) 369–5912._

**Walden Pond Reservation** lies on Route 126 just across Route 2 from Concord. It was here that Thoreau wrote _Walden_. Today a cairn marks the site of his cabin, and there is boating, fishing, swimming and a picnic ground.

Opening times and days vary with the season. Phone for details. The writers' houses, which all charge admission, are open daily from mid-April to October, from about 10am–5pm, Sunday usually from 1pm. The Lyceum also charges admission; it is open year round 10am–5pm, Sunday from 2pm. Walden Pond, open all year, is free but charges for parking.

# LEXINGTON

The village green, still surrounded by 18th-century buildings, has not changed much in appearance since 1775, when a line of Minutemen confronted a line of Redcoats. The British, planning to overawe the restive Colonials with a show of force, were marching from Boston to Concord to seize military supplies. But Paul Revere's midnight ride had alerted the Patriots, and the Minutemen mustered on the village green before dawn. The exact location of that fateful first skirmish on 19 April is marked with a statue of Captain John Parker, commander of the Minutemen. A boulder is inscribed with his command: 'Stand your ground. Don't fire unless fired upon, but if they mean to have a war, let it begin here.' A shot was fired, no one knows by whom, and eight of the 77 Minutemen were killed. The best place to start a visit is at the Lexington Visitors Center, with its maps, brochures and diorama of the battle of Lexington.
*1875 Massachusetts Avenue. Tel: (617) 862-1450. Open: May to October, daily 9am–5pm; rest of the year, 9am–3.30pm. Free.*

## Buckman Tavern

Next to the Visitors Center is Buckman Tavern, where the Minutemen waited through the night after Paul Revere's warning. The tavern, built in 1709, looks exactly as it did in April 1775. Costumed guides give tours of the building.
*Hancock Street. Tel: (617) 862-5598. Open: mid-April to October, Monday to Saturday 10am–5pm, Sunday from 1pm. Admission charge.*

## Hancock-Clark House

John Hancock's father built this house in 1700. It was here that Sam Adams and

John Hancock hid after being warned of the British advance by Paul Revere. Both men were wanted by the British for their opposition to the Crown.
*36 Hancock Street. Tel: (617) 861-0928. Open: mid-April to October, Monday to Saturday 10am–5pm, Sunday from 1pm. Admission charge.*

## Munroe Tavern

The Munroe Tavern served as field headquarters and hospital for the British in their retreat from Concord. It has been restored to its original appearance.

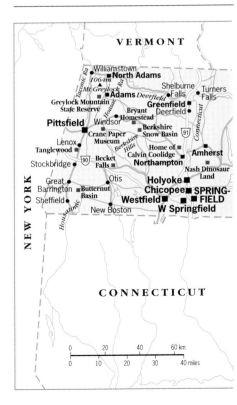

Lexington's First Parish Church

*1332 Massachusetts Avenue. Tel: (617) 862-1703. Open: mid-April to October, Monday to Saturday 10am–4pm, Sunday from 1pm. Admission charge.*

## Museum of Our National Heritage

This modern brick and glass building has displays illustrating the country's history from Colonial times to the present day. Permanent exhibits include swords, clocks and furniture from different eras. Weekly programmes include films and concerts.

*Route 2A and Massachusetts Avenue. Tel: (617) 861-6560. Open: Monday to Saturday 10am–5pm, Sunday from noon. Free.*

# MASSACHUSETTS

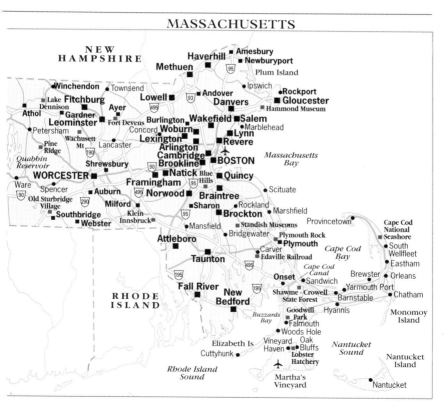

# Literary New England

*T*he literary heritage of the Northeast goes back to Benjamin Franklin, who published *Poor Richard's Almanac* in the 1700s. New England was an obvious home for writers, having both the cultural background of Europe and the first printing press in the New World.

Early in the 19th century Boston's Edgar Allen Poe developed a genre of mystery and horror literature that has continued to gain in popularity, with authors like Stephen King carrying on the tradition. Later, the Transcendental movement became popular. They believed in the mystical union of all nature and based themselves around Concord, Massachusetts. Ralph Waldo Emerson wrote his essays on nature there and befriended Henry David Thoreau, whose *Walden* has become an American classic on environmentalism.

Louisa May Alcott's family lived in Concord, and it was here she wrote her most famous novel, *Little Women.* Nathaniel Hawthorne bought the Alcott family home. He was an influence on Herman Melville, who lived in Pittsfield, in the Berkshires of western Massachusetts, where he wrote the classic *Moby Dick.* In Hartford, Connecticut, Harriet Beacher Stowe and Mark Twain were close neighbours on Nook Farm. Twain wrote both *Huckleberry Finn* and *The Adventures of Tom Sawyer* from his home there.

Nobel Prize winner Eugene O'Neill is universally acknowledged as America's greatest dramatist, and it was with the Provincetown Players, on Cape Cod, that he produced the work that led to his Pulitzer Prize in 1920.

New England has also had more than its fair share of great poets. Henry Wadsworth Longfellow was born in Maine and became a professor of literature at Harvard. The reclusive Emily Dickinson lived in Amherst, Massachusetts, and Robert Frost lived on a New Hampshire farm for several years and then spent his summers in Vermont. Other notable New England poets include e e cummings (by convention his name is spelt this way) and Amy Lowell.

In the late 18th century Henry James wrote both *The Europeans* and *The Bostonians* based on his New England experiences. More recently, both *Couples*, by John Updike, and *The Hotel New Hampshire*, by John Irving, are very much New England novels. Norman Mailer studied at Harvard and developed strong ties with the area.

Gloucester's memorial to drowned seafarers

THEY THAT GO DOWN TO THE SEA IN SHIPS

Rockport, famed for its scenery and for the shops, restaurants and galleries of Bearskin Neck

## THE NORTH SHORE

The North Shore of Massachusetts is an unspoiled stretch of rugged coast and seaports that has escaped excessive commercialisation.

### GLOUCESTER

Gloucester, 40 miles northeast of Boston, is the oldest fishing port in the nation, and fishing continues to be the town's main industry. On Western Avenue stands the famous Fishermen's Memorial, _Man at the Wheel_, in memory of '[them] that go down to the sea in ships'. Harbour tours and narrated whale-watch cruises are available from the wharfs.

_Cape Ann Chamber of Commerce (main information centre on the North Shore), Commercial Street. Tel: (978) 283–1601._

### MARBLEHEAD

The protected harbour at Marblehead, 18 miles northeast of Boston, attracted fishermen from Cornwall, who settled here in 1629. The harbour is one of New England's most popular among today's pleasure sailors. Several very fine 17th- and 18th-century houses line the winding streets of the old part of town. Historic sights include **Abbot Hall**, the old town hall in Washington Square (tel: 781 631–0528), and the **Jeremiah Lee Mansion** at 161 Washington Street (tel: 617 631–1069).

_Chamber of Commerce, 62 Pleasant Street. Tel: (781) 631–2868._

### ROCKPORT

A few minutes north of Gloucester, on Route 127, is one of the most painted and photographed harbours in America (a lobster shack here has earned the nickname 'Motif No 1'). It is certainly picturesque and has become almost an icon for the New England fishing port.

Rockport itself is a charming fishing village on the rocky promontory of Cape Ann. Long a favourite with tourists, it has nevertheless been developed with restraint and good taste, and its quaint atmosphere retained.

_Chamber of Commerce, 3 Main Street. Tel: (978) 546–6575._

With grim zealotry Salem's citizens executed 14 women, six men and two dogs for witchcraft

## SALEM

A few miles north of Marblehead, on Route 1A, is one of America's most infamous towns. Founded in 1626 by Roger Conant, Salem became the most Puritan of Puritan towns. Roger Williams was driven from here for his liberal beliefs and went on to found Rhode Island. The zealots of Salem continued to purge the town of perceived evildoers, leading to the witchcraft hysteria of 1692 (see box).

But there is far more to the town than gruesome executions. Salem went on to become a major trading port and seafaring centre. During the late 1700s ships began trading with China and the Far East, and this led to the birth of the China trade.

### ESSEX INSTITUTE

A visit to this group of historic houses, library, art gallery and museum gives a good introduction to the history of Salem. Visit the three beautifully restored houses in chronological order to get a feel for the changes in lifestyle over 150 years – the **John Ward House** built in 1685, the **Crowninshield-Bentley House** dating back to 1727, and the **Garneer-Pingree House** of 1805. *132 Essex Street. Tel: (978) 744-3390. Open: Monday to Saturday 10am–5pm, Sunday noon–5pm. Closed: Monday from November until June. Admission charge.*

### HOUSE OF THE SEVEN GABLES HISTORIC SITE

Nathaniel Hawthorne immortalised this 1668 house in his novel of the same name. It has been restored to its appearance in Hawthorne's time, and a film describes how the house inspired him to write his novel. Also on the grounds are three other historic houses, period gardens and panoramic views of Salem Harbor.

*54 Turner Street. Tel: (978) 744–0991. Open: daily 10am–5pm, Sunday from noon. Admission charge.*

## PEABODY ESSEX MUSEUM

The Peabody Essex Museum is the oldest museum in continuous operation in the United States. It was founded in 1799 as the East India Marine Society, to exhibit 'natural and artificial curiosities' that had been collected on their voyages around the world.

There are four major collections in the museum, all of them related to maritime matters and international commerce. Over 300,000 items are housed in seven buildings with over 30 galleries. The Asian Export Art Collection is a unique collection of objects that were made in Asia for export between 1500 and 1940. There is a maritime history collection, a natural history exhibit and an ethnology collection with pottery, jewellery, clothing and musical instruments from Japan, China, Korea, India and the Pacific. The Japanese collection is one of the most important in the world.

*East India Square. Tel: (978) 744–3390. Open: Monday to Saturday 10am–5pm, Sunday noon–5pm. Admission charge.*

## SALEM MARITIME NATIONAL HISTORIC SITE

This includes the 2,000-foot-long Derby Wharf, the Bonded Warehouse and the Custom House (immortalised in *The Scarlet Letter*). The West India Goods Store sells items similar to those on sale in 19th-century Salem, such as coffee, tea, spices and porcelain.

*174 Derby Street waterfront. Tel: (978) 740–1660. Open: daily 9am–5pm. Closed: New Year's Day, Thanksgiving and Christmas Day. Admission charge.*

Re-enacted trials at the Witch Dungeon Museum reveal Puritanism's fatal fanaticism

## SALEM WITCH MUSEUM

Set in an 1840s church, the museum graphically recounts the chronology of the witch hunt in an elaborate sound and light show with 13 life-size tableaux. Children love this macabre exhibit.

*19½ Washington Square North. Tel: (978) 744–1692. Open: daily 10am–5pm; July and August 10am–7pm. Admission charge.*

## THE WITCH HOUSE

This 1642 dwelling was the home of Judge Jonathan Corwin, who presided at the witch trials. The interior has been restored to its appearance in 1692, when over 200 women accused of witchcraft were brought here to the judge's chamber.

*310 Essex Street. Tel: (978) 744–0180. Open: daily 10am–4.30pm; March to June 10am–6pm; July and August 10am–4.30pm. Admission charge.*

# South Shore and Cape Cod

*T*he Pilgrims were the first settlers on the Cape in 1620. Access was always difficult, and this prevented the development of mass tourism until a road to Provincetown was completed in 1938. Cape Cod was never the same again. It has achieved an almost mythical reputation as an idyllic seaside destination, which attracts almost four million tourists every summer. Before June and after August the area returns to a more leisurely pace, and the wild beaches can be experienced in something like their natural state. The jewels of the Cape are the islands of Nantucket and Martha's Vineyard, reached by ferry from Hyannis or Woods Hole, or by air for short domestic connections. Both islands are small enough for a day trip.

## BREWSTER

There used to be several interesting attractions for children all along Route 6A (which in Brewster becomes Main Street), but this has been reduced to two. The **Cape Cod Museum of Natural History** has a working beehive, nature trails and a weather station. The **New England Fire and History Museum** has displays of old fire-fighting equipment dating from the late 1700s accompanied by the sounds of old firebells and alarms, plus a Victorian apothecary shop, herb garden and blacksmith shop.

*Cape Cod Museum, Route 6A. Tel: (508)*

The refreshing simplicity of a beach curving along Nantucket Sound, Martha's Vineyard

*896–3867. Open: Monday to Saturday, 9.30am–4.30pm, Sunday from 12.30pm. Admission charge.*
*Fire and History Museum, Route 6A. Tel: (508) 896–5711. Open: Monday to Friday, 10am–4pm, Saturday and Sunday from noon. Admission charge.*

## EASTHAM

**Cape Cod National Seashore** stretches from Orleans all the way to the far northern tip of the Cape. Some 27,000 acres of dunes, glacial cliffs, woods, marshes and ponds have an extensive network of nature trails and bicycle trails giving access to this wild coastal landscape.

The Salt Pond Visitors Center, on Nauset Bay near Eastham, has plenty of literature on the Seashore, together with maps and trail guides. Guided walks and lectures are offered.
*Exit 18 off Route 6A. Tel: (508) 255–3421. Open: all year (seashore); daily early March to 2 January (visitor center). Free (parking charge).*

## MARTHA'S VINEYARD

Martha's Vineyard is one of the most fashionable summer retreats in America (see pages 80–1). Jackie Onassis had a house here, as do many entertainment celebrities, and although the island is only 20 miles long by 10 miles wide, the famous faces manage to avoid the 65,000 visitors that come over every summer.

The island is undeniably attractive. Picture-perfect small towns like Edgartown sit in scenery reminiscent of the Irish coast. Commercialism has by and large been avoided, and the only major concessions to tourism are the mopeds that buzz around the island like angry bees, much to the annoyance of residents.

## NANTUCKET

The island of Nantucket, 30 miles off the Massachusetts mainland, is more remote and even smaller and less developed than Martha's Vineyard. The town of Nantucket (see pages 82–3) has an old-world charm that has been preserved to perfection. Outside the main town there is a village at either end of the island; Madaket to the west and Siasconset, which is particularly attractive, to the east. There are good beaches all round the island.

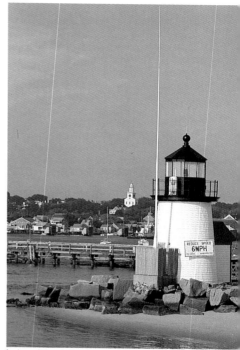

A sign of the civilised pace of life on Nantucket, 30 miles out to sea from Cape Cod

### DRIVING THE CAPE

Cape Cod is, technically speaking, an island by virtue of the Cape Cod Canal, which effectively separates the arm of the Cape from the mainland. Route 6 crosses the canal on the Sagamore Bridge and continues on to Provincetown at the far tip of the Cape. Route 28 crosses the Bourne Bridge and continues to Falmouth and points along the south shore. This is the road to take to catch the ferry to Martha's Vineyard.

The best way to approach Cape Cod is on Route 6A. This introduction is both more attractive and more in keeping with the mood of the Cape than the southern route. Route 28 through Hyannis consists of cheap motels alternating with fast-food outlets and gas stations. Hardly appealing as first impressions go!

Route 6A splits off from Route 6 shortly after crossing the Sagamore Bridge. A string of charming small towns like Sandwich, Yarmouth and Brewster line its north shore.

## PLYMOUTH

Plymouth lies just off the main road from Boston to Cape Cod, and on no account should the short detour be missed. The town is full of early American history (see pages 84–5), and visitors can gain a remarkable insight into the lives of the Pilgrims.

### Cranberry World

Plymouth and Cape Cod are the habitat for one of America's native fruits, the cranberry, which grows in low-lying bogs. Every September and early October, when the bogs are flooded, lakes of brilliant red cranberries colour

A red tide of cranberries at Carver during harvest time

the countryside. **Ocean Spray's Cranberry World** has exhibits of equipment, historic photographs and a small working cranberry bog – plus opportunities to sample their products. If the cranberry theme catches your imagination, drive along Route 58 about 10 miles to Carver, cranberry capital of the world. In the autumn there are cranberries as far as the eye can see.
*225 Water Street. Tel: (508) 747–2350. Open: daily 9.30am–5pm May to November. Free.*

### The *Mayflower II*

In 1620 the original *Mayflower* made the voyage from England in 66 days. The three-masted merchant vessel had previously been in the fish trade with Norway and, after that, in the wine trade with France. The 102 passengers, Puritan refugees from religious intolerance, left England and 102 arrived in the New World – one dying at sea and one being born (appropriately named Oceanus Hopkins).

The full-scale reproduction of the original *Mayflower* made the eventful 44-day voyage from England in 1957 under full sail. The *Mayflower II* now sits in Plymouth Harbor, where you can talk with guides about the history of Plymouth Colony, life on board the original *Mayflower*, wooden ship-building and the ongoing restoration of *Mayflower II*. Entering the ship you can browse through exhibits about New England's native people and the voyage of the *Mayflower II* from England.
*State Pier. Tel: (508) 746–1622. Open: daily 9am–5pm. Closed: December to March. Admission charge.*

### Plimoth Plantation

Three miles south of the *Mayflower II*

Folk at Plimoth Plantation pass the time of day along a dusty, straw-strewn road

lies Plimoth Plantation, a site that is almost totally isolated from the 20th century (the only intrusion being the occasional aircraft flying overhead).

From the Visitor Center, the walk to the actual settlement takes several minutes, but the effect is remarkable. Once the car park and modern buildings of the Visitor Center are well out of sight and sound, the path rounds a corner into an unpaved street. Suddenly it is 1627. A complete village, authentic in every detail, descends down the slope towards the sea. Chickens run about, Pilgrims tend gardens and work on the buildings, the women often wear corsets to give them the correct period shape. At lunch time, families sit around the table eating 17th-century meals cooked over wooden fires. The actor-interpreters speak in 17th-century English, and if it were not for all the 20th-century visitors the illusion would be complete. This is interpretive living history at its best.

Adjacent to the Plantation is **Hobbamock's Homesite**, a Wampanoag Indian home consisting of two simple shelters and two or three Indian interpreters who depict a very different culture from the Pilgrims', but in an equally lively and informative way. The settlement is within the Plimoth Plantation complex and does not require a separate entrance fee. The best times to visit Plimoth Plantation are early in the week either first thing in the morning or late in the afternoon. *Route 3A, Warren Avenue. Tel: (508) 746–1622. Open: daily 9am–5pm. Closed: December to March. Admission charge.*

## PROVINCETOWN

At the very northern tip of the Cape sits Provincetown, where the Pilgrims made their first landfall in 1620. A 252-foot Italianate tower commemorates the event and has a museum with, among other things, ship models, whaling equipment and salvage items. The **Pilgrim Monument**, as the tower is called, gives good views of Provincetown and the Cape.

After the Pilgrims came the whalers and fishermen, and Provincetown remains an active fishing port. Whale-hunting is still an active industry, although nowadays it is watching whales, rather than killing them, that makes the money; cruises leave from

Goblets, candlesticks and nursing bottles fill the sunlit shelves of Sandwich's Glass Museum

MacMillan Pier. There is also a visitor centre for Cape Cod National Seashore (see page 74); dune tours are conducted daily.

In the early 1900s, Provincetown was discovered by artists and writers, including playwright Eugene O'Neill. This love affair faded after tourists began frequenting the town in the 1940s. Today Provincetown is a mixture of interesting history and the worst elements of tourism. But it is worth persevering beyond the hamburger joints, T-shirt shops and cheap souvenir shops to encounter the old Provincetown that so charmed the artists. The Provincetown Chamber of Commerce has maps and brochures that list the address of every famous artist and writer who ever lived there.
*Chamber of Commerce, 307 Commercial Street. Tel: (508) 487–3424.*
*Monument, Town Hill, off Route 6. Tel: (508) 487–1310. Open: daily 9am–5pm, extended summer hours. Admission charge.*

## SANDWICH

Sandwich, situated at the western end of Route 6A, has more sights on the Cape than any other town. Slow growth has helped keep its original character intact. A lovely place, it is built around Shawme Pond, an artificial lake that provided water power for milling.

### Dexter's Gristmill

Next to the pond is a mill that was in use from the 1650s until the late 19th century; it is still used for practical demonstrations of old corn-milling techniques.
*Main Street. Open: mid-June to early October, Monday to Saturday 10am–5pm, Sunday from 1pm. Admission charge (with Hoxie House).*

## Heritage Plantation

These 76 acres of gardens to the east of Sandwich form one of the most ambitious historical complexes in New England. Formerly the estate of horticulturist Charles Dexter, who specialised in the propagation of rhododendrons, the gardens are a blaze of colour from mid-May to mid-June. Reproductions of historic buildings house several different collections. The **Vintage Car Museum**, in a replica of the famous round barn in Hancock Shaker Village (see page 88), has cars dating from 1890 to the beginning of World War II, including Gary Cooper's 1931 Duesenberg. Other buildings have displays of firearms, miniature military paintings, folk art and a 1912 carousel.
*At Grove and Pine Streets. Tel: (508) 888–3300. Open: mid-May to mid-October, daily 10am–5pm. Admission charge.*

## Hoxie House

Close to the mill is what claims to be the oldest house on the Cape (1637). This restored grey saltbox is complete with authentic 17th-century furnishings.
*Water Street. Tel: (508) 888–1173. Open: as for Dexter's Gristmill. Admission charge (with Dexter's Gristmill).*

## Sandwich Glass Museum

Deming Jarves founded the Boston and Sandwich Glass Company in the centre of the village in 1825. The materials he needed to operate efficiently and economically were here, and he believed his workers would be less distracted if they were away from the fleshpots of Boston. The formula worked. Sandwich glass, using a Roman three-part moulding method, became famous and is now highly valued by collectors for its subtle colours. The museum has an extensive collection of original pieces and

Ingenious Hoxie House: its chairs turn into tables, its beds into benches

a diorama illustrating glass-making.
*Town Hall Square. Tel: (508) 888–0251. Open: daily April to October 9.30am–4.30pm; rest of the year, Wednesday to Sunday 9.30am–4pm. Closed: January. Admission charge.*

## Thornton W Burgess Museum

Almost next door to Hoxie House is the small cottage that was home to the naturalist and author whose children's books included *Peter Cotton Tail* and *Old Mother West Wind*. The museum contains his writings, personal mementoes and original illustrations.
*4 Water Street. Tel: (508) 888–4668. Open: Monday to Saturday 10am–4pm, Sunday from 1pm. Closed: Easter, Thanksgiving and 25 December. Donation.*

# Martha's Vineyard

The island known as Martha's Vineyard is the ideal place to see by bicycle. There is an excellent network of bike paths, it is relatively flat apart from the Up-Island area, and it is small enough to cover in a day. The ferries carry cars as well as foot passengers, but during the summer it is far better, and cheaper, to leave cars on the mainland. Ferries arrive at either Vineyard Haven or Oak Bluffs, and several bike rental shops are visible as soon as you disembark. Rented mopeds (for which a driver's licence is required) are far from popular with the locals. *Allow 3 hours.*

## *1* VINEYARD HAVEN

This is the port most visitors use. A short walk from the docks, on Beach Road, is the Martha's Vineyard Chamber of Commerce (tel: 508 693–0085), with good maps and other information. Although never overly popular with tourists, the

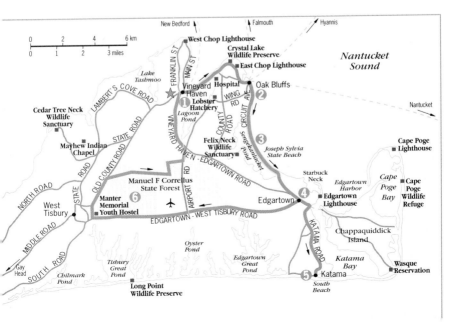

town has had a loyal following of writers since Lillian Hellman and Dashiell Hammett stayed here in the 1930s.
_Take Beach Road out of town and follow the coast past East Chop Lighthouse to Oak Bluffs._

## 2 OAK BLUFFS

Oak Bluffs was the first place on the island to become popular with tourists. The town is famous for the Oak Bluffs Campground, off Circuit Avenue, where there is a 33-acre cluster of Gothic Victorian holiday cottages.
_Take Sea View Avenue out of town past the town beach. A paved bike path follows the coast._

## 3 JOSEPH SYLVIA STATE BEACH

This sandy beach beside calm waters has good views towards Cape Cod, and there are always vendors with a varied assortment of fast food.
_Continue on the bike path._

## 4 EDGARTOWN

Edgartown is the most elegant town on the island, with expensive boutiques, fine restaurants and 17th- and 18th-century sea captains' houses. In Cooke Street, stop by the **Thomas Cooke House** (nothing to do with this book!), where the Dukes County Historical Society (tel: 508 627–4441) has historical background on the island and a walking-tour guide. The house itself is one of the Society's exhibits, illustrating the island's history through the eyes of a customs collector who lived here in the late 18th century.
_For an interesting side trip from Edgartown, take the bike path along Katama Road for about 3 miles to Katama Beach._

Eye-catching colour accentuates the Victorian detail of an Oak Bluffs cottage

## 5 KATAMA BEACH

Sometimes called South Beach, this has the best windsurfing on the island. Swimming can be dangerous on this 3-mile stretch of sand, but during the summer there are plenty of beach activities including informal sand-castle competitions.
_Return to Edgartown and take the Edgartown–West Tisbury Road._

## 6 MANUEL F CORRELLUS STATE FOREST

This cool, hushed forest in the centre of the island has almost 4,000 acres of pine, scrub oak, ponds and streams. A bike path, on which mopeds are prohibited, circles the forest. There is a 2-mile nature trail through the forest for those with enough energy.
_Continue around the forest on the bike path and take Airport Road to join the Vineyard Haven–Edgartown Road. Return to Vineyard Haven._

During the summer the narrow roads become very crowded. Be careful of both other traffic and loose gravel and sand. Every year there are cycling accidents on the island.

# Nantucket

In the 19th century Nantucket was the world capital of the whaling industry. But with the discovery of petroleum in 1859, demand for whale-oil plummeted, sending Nantucket into a slow decline that succeeded in preserving its character. It remains one of the most picturesque towns imaginable. The island's name came from the Indian word *nanticut*, meaning 'faraway land', and it still takes over two hours on the ferry from Hyannis. Even if only for a day, it is well worth a visit to this New England outpost.

*Leaving the Steamboat Wharf ferry terminal, walk down Broad Street to South Beach.*

### 1 WHALING MUSEUM
On the right-hand side of Broad Street, this old whale-oil candle factory now has displays relating to the history of whaling, including scrimshaw, harpoons, paintings and models. The crafts associated with the industry are also represented.

*Turn left into South Water Street and continue to Main Street.*

### 2 MAIN STREET SQUARE
This charming cobblestoned square is the heart of town, where it is easy to feel part of another century. Shops and galleries intermingle with old sea captains' homes.

### 3 PACIFIC CLUB
At the foot of the square, this old seamen's club (private) is still active as a place where mariners can tell tall tales or play a game of cribbage. The Chamber of Commerce at 48 Main Street has a good supply of literature and maps of the island.

*Walk up to Main Street.*

Summer strolling along a Nantucket street

## 4  MURRAY'S CLOTHING STORE

It was here that Rowland Macy left the family business, joined a whaling ship, went prospecting for gold in California and finally founded R H Macy & Co, one of America's biggest department store chains.

*Continue to 75 and 78 Main Street.*

## 5  HENRY AND CHARLES COFFIN HOUSES

These two wealthy brothers built identical houses facing each other. Charles was a simple Quaker, but notice the more flamboyant embellishments of Henry's house, particularly the cupola on the roof and the white marble trim round the front door.

*Continue to 93, 95 and 97 Main Street.*

## 6  THE THREE BRICKS

These three identical houses were built in the 1830s by Joseph Starbuck for his three sons. He retained the title to the houses to ensure that the sons stayed in the family business.

*Cross to 96 Main Street.*

## 7  HAWDEN HOUSE

This Greek Revival mansion is the only house on the tour open to the public. The elegant interior illustrates how wealthy 19th-century merchants lived (William Hawden was a merchant and candle-maker who owned the factory that now houses the Whaling Museum). Open during the summer only.

*Turn left into Pleasant Street, left into Summer Street and continue on to Moor's Lane; turn left into Fair Street.*

## 8  FAIR STREET MUSEUM

On the left, next to the Quaker Meeting House, this museum displays paintings of Nantucket by contemporary as well as

Viewing little Nantucket's historic houses, museums and galleries can occupy hours

19th-century artists. It is the art museum of the Nantucket Historical Association.

*Continue down Fair Street, turn right into Main Street and right again into Orange Street.*

## 9  UNITARIAN CHURCH

This 1809 building is one of the most beautiful on the island, and its golden dome has long been a landmark for seafarers. Notice the *trompe l'oeil* panelling inside.

*Return back along Main Street to Easy Street, then turn left back to Steamboat Wharf.*

# Plymouth

Few places in New England have so much authentic history concentrated into such a small area. This walk includes several historic houses dating back to the 16th and 17th centuries and all are open to the public. A route is suggested for the walk, but the sites are so close together that a leisurely day could be spent just wandering at random from museum to museum. *Allow 1½ hours, longer for museum visits.*

*Start on Water Street on the seafront.*

### 1 PLYMOUTH ROCK

What more suitable place could there be to begin than the point where the Pilgrims first set foot ashore in 1620? Plymouth Rock is enshrined in a neo-classical building that is considerably more impressive than the rock itself!
*Continue north on Water Street to State Pier.*

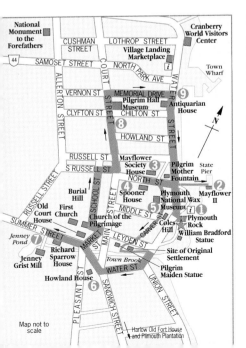

### 2 *MAYFLOWER II*

This is an accurate re-creation of the ship that brought the Pilgrims from England to New England. It is staffed by guides who talk about the history of Plymouth Colony, life on board the original *Mayflower*, wooden shipbuilding and the ongoing restoration of the *Mayflower II*.
*Cross Water Street and walk up North Street, past the Pilgrim Mother Fountain on the right, to Winslow Street.*

### 3 MAYFLOWER SOCIETY HOUSE

The tour of this house, built in 1754, covers two distinct periods. The front is authentic 1754 Colonial, while the rear is 1898 Victorian. Ralph Waldo Emerson was married here in 1835, and ether was discovered in this same house in 1842.
*Cross North Street.*

## 4 SPOONER HOUSE

The same family lived in this house for over 200 years, from 1749 to 1954. It is now a museum furnished with Spooner family heirlooms.
*Walk along North Street towards the sea and turn the corner into Carver Street.*

## 5 PLYMOUTH NATIONAL WAX MUSEUM

This is the only wax museum in New England, with 27 scenes depicting the Pilgrims' story.
*Cross Carver Street to Coles Hill, the original burial ground for the first settlers. Walk down the steps to Water Street, cross Leyden Street to Brewster Gardens and view the Pilgrim Maiden Statue. Follow the brook from Water Street and proceed to Sandwich Street.*

## 6 HOWLAND HOUSE

Members of the Pilgrim group once lived here. There are good displays of 17th- and 18th-century furnishings, and the house is staffed by costumed hostesses.
*Cross Pleasant Street to Summer Street and continue to Spring Lane.*

## 7 RICHARD SPARROW HOUSE

This 1640 house hosts demonstrations by local craftsmen in the craft shop.
*Walk down Market Street, then School Street, past the Burial Hill overlooking the harbour. Turn right into South Russell Street and left into Main Street, which turns into Court Street. Walk five blocks to Chilton Street.*

## 8 PILGRIM HALL MUSEUM

The nation's oldest public museum, built in 1824, houses the most complete collection of Pilgrim artefacts and possessions. There is the cradle of the first baby born in the new colony,

Plymouth Rock, the Pilgrims' stepping stone into the New World, sheltered in grand style

paintings by the Pilgrims, books, manuscripts and even household utensils.
*Walk down Memorial Drive.*

## 9 HEDGE HOUSE MUSEUM

An interesting costume and fashion display can be seen in this fine example of a merchant's home from the early 1800s. There are also several good examples of fine English china from the same period.
*Return to Plymouth Rock along Water Street.*

# Western Massachusetts

*T*wo major valleys extending from Vermont to Connecticut divide the western half of Massachusetts. The Pioneer Valley follows the course of the Connecticut River, and the Berkshire Valley follows the Housatonic River.

## AMHERST

Amherst, 25 miles north of Springfield, is an attractive, small academic community that is home to the University of Massachusetts, Hampshire College and Amherst College, as well as to both Noah Webster, of dictionary fame, and the poet Emily Dickinson. Amherst was founded in 1821, and its Victorian architecture lines the southern side of Amherst Common. With a student population of just 1,600, it is one of the smallest Ivy League colleges.
*Chamber of Commerce, 409 Main Street. Tel: (413) 253–0700.*

### Emily Dickinson House

Dickinson was born in this house and died here too. After her father's death in 1874, she left the house only once, when her nephew died next door. She wrote nearly 1,800 poems while she lived here, although only 10 were published during her lifetime. The rest, in neatly bound sheafs, were found by her sister after Emily's death in 1886.
*280 Main Street. Tel: (413) 542–8161. Open by appointment. Admission charge.*

### Mead Art Museum

The Mead has an excellent collection of 19th- and 20th-century American art, as well as artefacts, paintings and sculpture from the 17th to the 20th century.
*Amherst Campus, Route 116. Tel: (413) 542–2335. Open: Monday to Friday 10am–4.30pm, weekends 1–5pm; out of term, Tuesday to Sunday 1–4pm. Free.*

### Pratt Museum of Natural History

The museum has the world's largest mastodon skeleton, together with a large collection of local geological specimens.
*Amherst Campus, Route 116. Tel: (413) 542–2165. Open: Monday to Friday 9am–3.30pm, Saturday 10am–4pm, Sunday noon–5pm; out of term hours are limited, phone for information. Free.*

## DEERFIELD

Deerfield was settled in 1669 as a frontier outpost. In the Bloody Brook Massacre of 1675 the town lost 64 men in a fight with the Indians during King Philip's War. In 1704 the French led about 350 Indians on a dawn raid, killing 49 people in five hours, burning half the town and leading 112 prisoners on a winter death march to Canada. Settlers returned in 1706 and Deerfield developed into a small but prosperous agricultural centre.

### Historic Deerfield

This is considered one of the best-preserved Colonial districts in New England, and ranks with the greatest historic preservation areas in America. The first restoration project of its kind in the country, it consists of a single mile-long street (The Street), lined by 65 18th- and 19th-century houses, of which 12 are open to the public. Both the interiors and exteriors of the houses are completely authentic. A guided tour of the town's historic houses is the best way to experience Deerfield.

Risen from the ashes of 1675, Deerfield's present buildings are lovingly preserved

The **Ashley House** was the home of the Reverend John Ashley, who moved here in 1732, and contains a fine collection of 18th-century New England furniture.

One of the earliest dwellings is the 1720 **Frary House**, later converted to a tavern complete with ballroom and fiddlers' gallery.

The **Helen Geier Flynt Textile Museum** houses a collection of textiles, coverlets, needlework and clothing in an 1872 barn.

The **Henry N Flynt Silver and Metalware Collection** includes pieces by Paul Revere as well as English and American pewter and silver and a re-creation of an 18th-century silversmith's shop.

The **Sheldon-Hawks House** (1740) is one of the best-preserved 18th-century buildings. It has a good furniture collection and a beautifully restored kitchen.

The **Stebbins House** dates back to 1799 and was extended in 1810. It is notable for the exotic French wallpaper illustrating Captain Cook's South Sea voyages.

The **Wells-Thorn House** illustrates how life changed through increasing prosperity, with a series of seven rooms arranged chronologically from 1725 to 1850.

*Information Center, Hall Tavern. Tel: (413) 774–5581. Open: daily 9.30– 4.30pm. Closed: Thanksgiving and 25 December. Admission charge.*

### Memorial Hall Museum

The museum contains a collection of Colonial, Indian and military relics, as well as a replica of a 1797 schoolroom and a display of pewterware. A door still has a hatchet hole in it, a grim reminder of the fateful day of the French-led Indian raid.

*Memorial Street. Tel: (413) 774–7476. Open: May to October, daily 9.30am–4.30pm. Admission charge.*

## LENOX

South of Pittsfield, in the Berkshire Hills, is an area that became known as the 'Inland Newport' because of the extravagant 'cottages' built there by wealthy families. Many of these estates in Lenox and nearby Stockbridge (see page 92) are open to the public.

### The Mount

The Mount was the summer home of author Edith Wharton. The exquisite Gothic Revival mansion was built in 1902 and is currently undergoing major restoration, although it remains open to the public. Dramatic productions are presented here during summer.
*Plunket Street. Tel: (413) 637–1899.*
*Open: Memorial Day to end October, tours Tuesday to Sunday on the hour from 10am to 2pm. Times may vary if dramatic productions are offered.*

### Tanglewood

For many people Lenox is synonymous with Tanglewood, the summer home of the Boston Symphony Orchestra. Outdoor concerts are given on the beautiful, 210-acre estate during July and August.
*Hawthorne Road. Tel: (617) 266–1492 before mid-June, or (413) 637–1940 after mid-June.*

## PITTSFIELD
### Arrowhead

Just south of Pittsfield is Arrowhead, the home of Herman Melville, author of *Moby Dick*. From the study window there is a fine view of Mount Greylock, which reminded Melville of the great whale, Moby Dick.
*780 Holmes Road. Tel: (413) 442–1793.*
*Open: June to Labor Day, daily 10am–5pm; Labor Day to October, Friday to Monday 10am–5pm. Admission charge.*

### Hancock Shaker Village

This is one of the finest Shaker settlements in existence. The round barn built in 1826 is a masterpiece of functional design: one man standing at the centre of the barn could feed 54 cows at once. The village ceased being an active community in 1960, and since then 20 buildings have been restored. Interpreters demonstrate 19th-century skills such as woodworking, blacksmithing and Shaker cooking.
*US 20 (5 miles west of Pittsfield), junction of Routes 20 and 41. Tel: (413) 443–0188. Open: Memorial Day weekend to October, daily 9.30am–5pm; April, May, November 10am–3pm. Admission charge.*

## SPRINGFIELD

Springfield is a large industrial town that had one of the country's first motor car factories (1895). Nowadays the city's main claim to fame is the invention of basketball. The first game was played at Springfield College in 1891.

Ideals of simplicity and practicality are reflected in Shaker architecture and crafts

## Naismith Memorial Basketball Hall of Fame

The Basketball Hall of Fame honours the greatest players and coaches in the game, and captures basketball's excitement, from pro-to-amateur and from men-to-women. Visitors can view rare historic artefacts, play trivia games, watch films and buy souvenirs. Plenty of interactive exhibits, including the Spalding Shoot Out, where visitors can aim for baskets of different heights from a moving walkway.

*1150 West Columbus Avenue. Tel: (413) 781-6500. Open: daily 9.30am–5.30pm; July and August, Monday to Saturday 9am–7pm, Sunday 9.30am–5pm. Closed: Christmas, New Year's Day and Thanksgiving. Admission charge.*

## Nash Dinosaur Land

The Pioneer Valley was inhabited by over a hundred species of dinosaurs 200 million years ago. Geologist Careton Nash discovered dinosaur tracks here 50 years ago and has excavated extensively in what he calls the largest footprint quarry in the world. There is a small museum and shop adjoining the site.

*Route 116, South Hadley. Tel: (413) 467-9566. Open: daily 9am–5pm mid-April to mid-October; rest of year by appointment. Admission charge.*

## Riverside Park

In a suburb called Agawam ('crooked river') is one of the biggest amusement parks in New England. Riverside Park features the Cyclone, one of the country's largest roller-coasters, with more than 50 other exciting rides. On summer Saturday evenings, NASCAR (National Association of Stock Car Auto Racing) car racing is held here.

*1623 Main Street, Route 159, Agawam.*

Hancock's round Shaker barn, built in 1826, has the austere beauty of a masterpiece

*Tel: (413) 786-9300. Open: daily June to August 11am–midnight, Sunday till 11pm; weekends only September and October. Admission charge.*

### THE SHAKERS

The movement started in the north of England in 1747 as a branch of the Quaker religion. During church services, religious fervour caused their bodies to tremble and shake. They became known as the 'Shaking Quakers' and thus the 'Shakers'. In 1774 Ann Lee of Manchester, England, founder of the Shakers, ventured to the New World to escape religious persecution. She established the first Shaker community at Watervliet, New York.

# VILLAGES

The United States is a nation of cities. Provided they have an elected administration, even the smallest group of buildings calls itself a city and it is not just a question of semantics. Most settlements in this vast country, however small, have a distinctly urban atmosphere. New England is the notable exception.

It is only in New England that the European concept of a village exists at all, and nowhere in the US is the village more a part of everyday life.

Villages occur throughout the whole of New England, but it is in the northern states of Vermont, New Hampshire and Maine that they form the framework of the state with the occasional town thrown in to act as the administrative centre. Vermont, in particular, has enough villages of interest to keep a visitor busy for a month without ever venturing into one of the other New England states.

Most New England villages are developed according to a plan based around a central village green. Arranged around this green, or common, are a core of buildings that are essential to the life of every village. There is always a church, usually steepled, and almost always painted white. It is often called the meeting house. Alongside is the town hall, the village inn, the village store and the burial ground.

One of the joys of New England is

to travel the backroads and discover your own special village, but there are a few that deserve special mention.

Woodstock, Vermont, is a classic village, complete with covered bridge, that has grown way beyond its original size but still has all the atmosphere and characteristics of classic New England.

On a smaller scale is Weston,

From left to right: Vermont door with decorative broom; a typical village store in southern Vermont; red, white and blue at Peacham; wood house, wood fence, Woodstock

with a population of about 500, on Route 100, with classic village stores selling everything, from pot-bellied stoves to pickle barrels, facing each other on either side of the main street.

The Northeast Kingdom (see Vermont) is a mosaic of picturesque villages, but wherever you travel in New England the charm of the villages is inescapable.

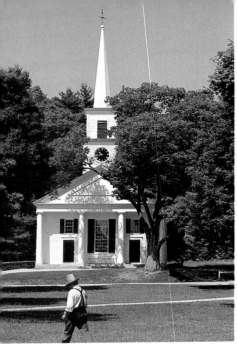

A Baptist church, built in 1832 in the Greek Revival style, faces Old Sturbridge Common

## STOCKBRIDGE

This tranquil Berkshire town is graced with a number of historic sites from the Colonial period and the 19th century. Its quaint character was captured by Norman Rockwell, the famed painter who spent the last 25 years of his life here (see States of the Arts, pages 132–3). As in nearby Lenox, the wealthy elite built summer 'cottages' here around the end of the last century.

### Chesterwood

This was the summer home and studio of monumental sculptor Daniel Chester French. The airy studio still contains clay models and plaster casts for many of his most famous works, including the Lincoln Memorial statue. A railroad track allowed him to roll sculptures outside to view in natural light.

*Off Route 183. Tel: (413) 298–3579.*
*Open: daily 10am–5pm May to October.*
*Admission charge.*

### Naumkeag

Stanford White designed this 23-room mansion in 1886 for New York lawyer Joseph Choate, Ambassador to England (1899–1905). It is an excellent example of the tastes of wealthy families of that era, and the landscaped grounds are particularly fine. In the house is an outstanding collection of Oriental porcelain and ceramics.
*Prospect Hill Road. Tel: (413) 298–3239.*
*Open: 10am–4.15pm Tuesday to Sunday from last week of June to August; weekends and holiday Mondays only, end of May to mid-June, September and October.*
*Admission charge.*

### Norman Rockwell Museum

This is the world's largest collection of the works of America's best-loved painter of small-town life. His red barn studio, displaying his easel and brushes just as he left them, was moved here from his home. Paintings include the famous *Four Freedoms*.
*Main Street. Tel: (413) 298–4100. Open: daily 10am–5pm. Closed: 1 and 18–31 January, Thanksgiving and 25 December. Admission charge.*

### STURBRIDGE

Imagine a typical rural village of the 1830s, spread out over 200 acres with farms, fields and gardens, and you have the re-created village of Old Sturbridge, 58 miles west of Boston. Some buildings were brought to Old Sturbridge from other parts of New England and carefully reconstructed; others are accurate reproductions – it is impossible to tell the difference.

Stop at the Visitor Center for maps and a 15-minute film on life in an early 19th-century village. Here you will also find the **J Cheney Wells Clock Gallery** (Wells was the founder of Old Sturbridge), which exhibits over a hundred American clocks made by New England clockmakers in the late 18th and early 19th centuries.

From the Visitor Center follow the path to the Common. The costumed guides all wear authentic period clothing – even down to the shoes, which are made by the shoemaker at his shop in the village. There is also a potter, glass-maker, weaver, printer, blacksmith, cooper and a working sawmill. Meals are served at the Bullard Tavern close to the covered bridge over the Quinebaug River. *Tel: (508) 347–3362. Open: daily 9am–5pm May to October. Closed: Mondays November to April. Admission charge.*

## WILLIAMSTOWN

Williamstown – a sleepy little town that is one of the most beautiful in all Massachusetts – is synonymous with

**Williams College**, one of the smallest Ivy League schools. The college dates from the late 18th century, and its elegant buildings are set round spacious lawns. Every summer the highly acclaimed Williamstown Theater Festival (tel: 413 597–3399) takes place on the college campus and attracts actors of international repute.

### Sterling and Francine Clark Art Institute

Surprisingly, one of the finest small art galleries in the country is located here. It has an exceptional collection of French Impressionists, including works by Monet, Renoir, Degas and Picasso. There are also paintings by American artists including Winslow Homer and John Singer Sargent and a small collection of furniture and silver. *225 South Street. Tel: (413) 458–9545. Open: 10am–5pm Tuesday to Sunday. Closed: 1 January, Thanksgiving and 25 December. Admission charge.*

Creeper-clad Williams College

# The Mohawk Trail

Officially designated Route 2, this road follows an old Pocumtuck Indian trail along the Deerfield and Cold Rivers. New England's first scenic road, opened in 1914, it starts in the Connecticut Valley and finishes in the Berkshire Hills. Many of the sites along its 60-mile stretch date back to the golden age of car touring. Autumn on the Mohawk Trail is particularly spectacular. *Allow 2 hours.*

*Starting in Greenfield, drive west under Interstate 91. On the right-hand side, soon after heading uphill, there is the Longview Gift Shop and Tower from which, for a nominal fee, you can look out over five states. Continue climbing until the road levels out, passing farms, tiny villages and Indian trading posts. Continue to Shelburne.*

## 1 GOULD'S SUGAR HOUSE
Seven miles out of Greenfield, this traditional sugar house still collects maple sap in buckets and uses a wood fire to boil the sap down to syrup. The best time to visit is during March when the sap is flowing, but the delicious syrup can be tasted all year in the adjoining restaurant.
*Continue along Route 2 and take the first left turn into Shelburne Falls.*

## 2 SHELBURNE FALLS
Potholes formed during the last Ice Age can be seen close to

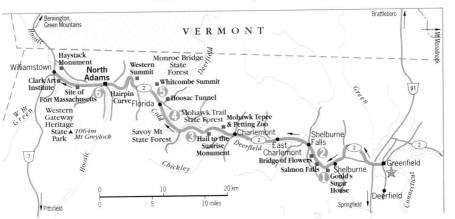

Salmon Falls, on the riverbank near Deerfield Avenue. Also of interest is the Bridge of Flowers, a former trolley bridge that is now an aerial flower garden. Of several good craft shops, one of the most interesting is North River Glass on Deerfield Avenue, where glass-making is demonstrated.

*Return to Route 2 and turn left. Continue through Charlemont. There are good views of the Deerfield river and several good picnic stops. On the right is the Mohawk Tepee and Petting Zoo.*

### 3 HAIL TO THE SUNRISE MONUMENT

On the left leaving town, a statue of an Indian raising his hands to the sky stands proudly on a 9-ton boulder. It was erected in 1932 in honour of the Five Indian Nations of the Mohawk Trail. A pool in front has 100 stones inscribed by tribes and councils from all over America.

*Getting more rugged and mountainous, the road narrows and enters a densely wooded area. On the right is a vehicle entrance to the forest.*

### 4 MOHAWK TRAIL STATE FOREST

A bridge over the Deerfield River leads to a fee-paying area with basic recreational facilities including a campground and picnic area. Free parking is available on the right before crossing the bridge, and there are many trails through the forest and along

Gould's Sugar House, Mohawk Trail, Shelburne. Tel: (413) 625–6170.
Mohawk Trail Association, PO BOX J, Charlemont, MA 01339.
Mohawk Trail State Forest, Route 2. Tel: (413) 339–5504.

the river that start from here.

*Continue up the steep road through beautiful forest scenery. Pass through the village of Florida, with its picturesque church, and continue to Whitcombe Summit.*

### 5 WHITCOMBE SUMMIT

The lookout tower gives good views of Mount Greylock, Mount Monadnock, in New Hampshire and the Green Mountains in Vermont. The adjoining motel offers 100-mile views from every room.

*Continue along the winding road enjoying panoramic views. At Western Summit, look out over the Hoosac Valley; at Hairpin Curve the view stretches from the Hoosac Valley to the Berkshire Valley and the Taconic Range. The road winds steeply down.*

### 6 NORTH ADAMS

This is an industrial town with several fine red-brick 19th-century mills.

*Route 2 continues on to Williamstown and into New York State.*

Indians once used the Trail as an invasion route

# Connecticut

*A*fter Massachusetts, Connecticut is the most developed state in New England. It is also the second smallest – only minuscule Rhode Island is smaller. Along the Massachusetts border Connecticut is still very rural, but from Hartford to Long Island Sound the state is much more developed.

Connecticut became the most industrialised state in New England largely because the glacial soil that covers much of the state is just too poor to support crops. Commerce and manufacturing were the means by which the economy grew, and it has become one of the most productive states in the country. Early industries included brass manufacture, firearms (the Colt 45 was developed here), clocks and textiles.

The state was founded by Puritans who felt that Massachusetts was becoming too liberal for their taste. In 1633 they founded three towns by the Connecticut River – Hartford, Wethersfield and Windsor. These were joined together as the Hartford Colony in 1639, and a document called 'The Fundamental Orders of Connecticut' was drawn up as a basis for government, the world's first written constitution. Today Connecticut's nickname, The Constitution State, is on every car licence plate.

## BRIDGEPORT

Bridgeport was the home of showman and circus proprietor P T Barnum. In 1891 he willed that a museum be built in the city centre, and the museum is as eccentric as he was. It has three floors of circus memorabilia including the costumes and furniture belonging to Tom Thumb, a 28-inch-tall man who was Barnum's first major attraction. There is also a 1,000-square-foot model of a three-ring circus, with over 3,000 miniature hand-carved figures.
*820 Main Street. Tel: (203) 331–9881. Open: Tuesday to Saturday 10am–4.30pm, Sunday from noon. Closed: holidays. Admission charge.*

## CHESTER

Located on Route 154, Chester is another charming village on the way to the ferry which crosses to the east bank of the Connecticut River (see below). The 5-minute crossing operates

---

### THE CONNECTICUT VALLEY

This valley follows the longest waterway in New England. A good road follows the river, linking the major sites; alternatively, there are boat trips on the river, including a ferry from Long Island to Haddam.

The Connecticut River Valley and Shoreline Visitors Council (393 Main Street, Middletown, tel: 800 486–3346) is the best place to start, with a mass of information and detailed maps. There is also an information centre on Route 95 at Westbrook.

Route 154 meanders through Old Saybrook, a picturesque town that was the original home of Yale University. It has views over both the Sound and the mouth of the Connecticut River. From here the road winds through salt marshes and hugs the river as far as Essex. (Route 9 provides a faster way to Essex.)

throughout the day from April to November at a nominal charge. Crossing the river, you will see the silhouette of Gillette Castle (see **Hadlyme**, page 99) rising up on the hillside straight ahead.

**EAST HADDAM**

At East Haddam the **Goodspeed Opera House** has been restored to its former Victorian glory on the riverbank. It even has its own dock, which harks back to Victorian times when many of the audience arrived by boat. The splendid four-storey opera house is open for tours; during the summer, musical revivals are performed nightly.

Also in East Haddam is a little red schoolhouse where Nathan Hale taught for two years before he was hanged as a spy by the British.

Riverboat named after a Mark Twain character on the Connecticut River near East Haddam

*Goodspeed Opera House, Route 82. Tel: (860) 873–8668.*

# CONNECTICUT

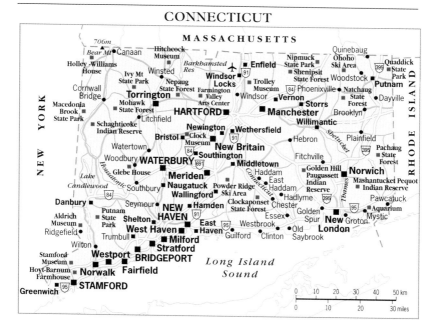

Bed-and-breakfast inns, like this one in Essex, can be found throughout New England

## ESSEX

Essex was settled in 1645 and became a major shipbuilding centre. America's first warship, the *Oliver Cromwell*, was built here in 1775. With its tree-lined streets and white clapboard houses, the village has lost none of its old-world charm. On summer weekends it seems that all the boats in Connecticut converge here; a midweek visit is more relaxed.

### Connecticut River Museum

This has a full-size replica of the first submarine, called *The Turtle*, built in 1775 by a local man. There is also a model of the *Oliver Cromwell*, together with other nautical exhibits.
*Main Street. Tel: (860) 767–8269. Open: year-round, Tuesday to Sunday 10am–5pm. Closed: Labor Day, Thanksgiving and 25 December. Admission charge.*

### Steam Train and Riverboat

Follow the Connecticut River Valley in an old-fashioned steam train (first-class available), then connect with an optional riverboat cruise (2 hours total).
*Valley Railroad, west of exit 3 off Route 9. Open: May to December. Admission charge.*

## GROTON AND NEW LONDON

Beside the Thames River lies the US Naval Submarine Base at Groton. Several submersible craft are on display including *The Turtle*, the world's first prototype submarine. The craft failed to operate successfully but became the model for submarines of the future. The highlight of the base is the USS *Nautilus*, the world's first nuclear-powered submarine. The *Nautilus* is permanently moored here and is classified as a National Historic Landmark.
*Route 12. Tel: (800) 343–0079. Open: year-round, daily 9am–5pm; Closed: Tuesday during November to May. Free.*

### Coastguard Academy Museum

Across the Thames River from Groton, in New London, is the US Coast Guard Academy. Do not be deceived – there is plenty of interest, even for landlubbers. The museum has extensive displays on the history of the Coast Guard. The Visitors Center also has displays on Coast Guard history and life as a cadet. The most impressive exhibit, when it is in port, is the *Eagle*, a three-masted square-rigged training ship built in 1936, which carries cadets to Europe and the Caribbean. It is a beautiful sight sailing out to sea down the Thames.
*Mohegan Avenue, Route 32, New London. Tel: (860) 444–8270. Open: daily 9am–5pm. Free.*

## HADDAM

This little Colonial town, bisected by the Connecticut River, lies on Route 154. Settled in 1662, it was an important fishing and trading port. It is now home to the New England Steamboat Lines, which cruise the Connecticut River and round the coast to Block Island, Martha's Vineyard and Nantucket.

# HADLYME

**Gillette Castle** has a medieval look but was built in 1919. William Gillette, an actor/playwright who became famous portraying Sherlock Holmes, designed and decorated the idiosyncratic 24-room building. Mirrors in his bedroom allowed him to see who was downstairs, so that he could decide when to be 'indisposed'. It is now the centrepiece of a state park.

*67 River Road, Hadlyme. Tel: (860) 526–2336. Open: June to mid-October, daily 10am–5pm; mid-October to December, weekends only to 4pm. Admission charge.*

A 55-minute journey by steam train from Essex connects with an optional river cruise

## HARTFORD

The high-rise buildings of modern Hartford reflect the importance of trade and commerce to Connecticut's state capital. They also hide the fact that this is one of New England's most historic cities. Originally a Dutch trading post, it became an English settlement in 1635; in 1662, the Colony of Connecticut was established. During the 1700s the city was an important shipbuilding and world trade centre. It later became the insurance capital of the world. Today Hartford is a pleasant city with just enough history left to make a short visit worthwhile.

### Mark Twain House

Nook Farm was a neighbourhood in the Hartford suburbs when Mark Twain built his mansion there in 1874. It was here that he wrote most of his best-known works, including *Tom Sawyer* and *Huckleberry Finn*. The house has been skilfully restored and contains a large collection of Twain memorabilia (tel: (860) 493–6411).

Next to the Twain House is the home of Harriet Beecher Stowe, author of *Uncle Tom's Cabin*. The house has much of its original furniture and several paintings by the writer.
*351 Farmington Avenue. Tel: (860) 525–9317. Open: daily 9.30am–4pm, Sunday 11am–4pm. Closed: Tuesday, January to May and October to November. Admission charge.*

### Old State House

A Federal-style building designed in 1792 by Charles Bulfinch, this was the first state house in the newly independent United States. The building sits in the downtown district surrounded by modern office blocks; it was saved from bulldozing only by the perseverance of conservationists. Most of the Old State

The Senate Chamber of the Old State House displays a portrait of George Washington

House is a museum. The visitors centre inside the building can provide free walking maps of the city centre area.
*800 Main Street. Tel: (860) 522–6766. Open: Monday to Friday 10am–4pm, Saturday 11am–4pm. Free.*

### State Capitol
The State Capitol stands prominently above Bushnell Park. It is a classic of Victorian civic architecture, with an interior as flamboyant as the golden-domed exterior.
*Capitol information desk and tour guide service, tel: (860) 240–0222.*

### Wadsworth Atheneum
A short distance from the Old State House is America's oldest public art gallery. The Wadsworth Atheneum houses an excellent eclectic collection of art from Rembrandt and Caravaggio to Williem de Kooning and Frank Stella. Both the French Impressionists and the Hudson School are particularly well represented. There is also a fine collection of early American furniture, tools and household utensils and the Hammerslough collection of silver.
*600 Main Street. Tel: (860) 278–2670. Open: Tuesday to Sunday 11am–5pm. Admission charge. Thursdays free.*

### LITCHFIELD
The town of Litchfield is one of the most attractive Colonial villages in New England. A white-steepled church, built in 1829, stands by a sprawling village green which dates back to 1770. Around the green, on beautiful tree-lined streets, are houses and shops dating back as far as the early 1700s. The Litchfield Hills have become highly fashionable, and a sought-after address among New York celebrities wanting a weekend retreat.

Experience New England's seafaring past in the living maritime museum of Mystic Seaport

### MYSTIC
During the 19th century, Mystic was one of New England's busiest seaports. Today it is synonymous with **Mystic Seaport**, a re-creation of a 19th-century seaport, covering 17 acres of riverfront. There is a children's museum, church, schoolhouse, bank, pharmacy, several shops where craftsmen carve figureheads or work on scrimshaw, a huge shipyard where wooden sailing ships are worked on, and over 300 ships moored at the village docks, including a wooden whaler. Horse-and-carriage rides and river cruises aboard a steamboat are available.
*75 Greenmanville Avenue. Tel: (860) 572–5315. Open: daily year-round; spring to fall 9am–5pm, summer 9am–6pm, winter 10am–4pm. Admission charge.*

### Mystic Marinelife Aquarium
This has 48 indoor exhibits, outdoor exhibits of seals, sea lions and penguins, and a 1,400-seat theatre that hosts sea lion, dolphin and whale shows.
*Coogan Boulevard. Tel: (860) 572–5955. Open: daily 9am–5pm. Admission charge.*

Roseland Cottage, tucked away in a part of Quiet Corner

## NEW HAVEN

New Haven is home to one of America's finest universities. Yale is like an oasis in the middle of a neglected 19th-century residential development. The campus of fine old buildings fronting on to green quadrangles proclaims itself to be a venerable academic institution.
*Campus tours available through the Visitor Information Center, 14 Elm Street. Tel: (203) 432–2300.*

### Peabody Museum of Natural History

This has an outstanding Hall of Dinosaurs, with a 65-foot brontosaurus skeleton, and zoology, mineralogy and meteorite exhibits.
*170 Whitney Avenue. Tel: (203) 432–5050. Open: Monday to Saturday 10am–5pm, Sunday from 12pm. Closed: major holidays. Admission charge.*

### Yale Center for British Art

Paintings, drawings, prints, books and sculptures survey British art from Elizabethan times to the present.
*1080 Chapel Street. Tel: (203) 432–2800. Open: Tuesday to Saturday 10am–5pm,*
*Sunday from 12pm. Closed: major holidays. Free.*

### Yale Collection of Musical Instruments

Over 800 instruments are featured illustrating 400 years of development. Concerts are given periodically.
*15 Hillhouse Avenue. Tel: (203) 432–0822. Open: September to May, Tuesday to Thursday 1–4pm; June, Tuesday and Thursday 1–4pm. Closed: July and August and major holidays. Free.*

### Yale University Art Gallery

This is the oldest university art museum in the Western Hemisphere, founded in 1832. It exhibits a variety of classical and contemporary works.
*1111 Chapel Street. Tel: (203) 432–0600. Open: Tuesday to Saturday 10am–5pm, Sunday from 2pm. Closed: major holidays. Free.*

## NORWICH

The most interesting feature in this small industrial town is the Leffingwell Inn. Started in 1675, Thomas Leffingwell bought it in 1770 and opened it as an inn. He subsequently added rooms to extend the inn to its present size. George Washington visited the inn several times during the Revolution, and it has been restored to its appearance at that time. *348 Washington Street. Tel: (860) 889–9440. Open: mid-May to mid-October, Tuesday to Sunday 2–4pm. Admission charge.*

## QUIET CORNER

The northeast corner of Connecticut seems to have been locked in an earlier age, and its 'Quiet Corner' nickname has certainly been well earned. Few tourists venture into these parts, and there are no towns of any size. The landscape is peaceful and pastoral, but there are a few sites of interest.

Open daily from 9am–5pm is **Caprilands Herb Farm** (Silver Street, Coventry, off Route 44 – tel: 860 742–7244). It has 31 herb gardens to wander through at no charge, including one that has all the herbs mentioned in Shakespeare.

**Roseland Cottage** in Woodstock provides one of the finest examples of Gothic Revival architecture (Route 169, tel: 860 928–4074). It is open from June to mid-October, Wednesday to Sunday 11am–5pm. Admission charge.

## WETHERSFIELD

The suburb of Wethersfield, about 10 miles out of Hartford, was one of the original three settlements of the Hartford Colony. Unlike Hartford, Wethersfield retains an extensive historic district, with over 150 houses that predate 1850.

### Buttolph-Williams House

Built in 1692, this simple Colonial structure has served as a dwelling house for over 250 years. The interior is complete with period furniture, pewter and 17th-century household items. *249 Broad Street. Tel: (860) 529–0460. Open: May to October, Wednesday to Monday 10am–4pm. Closed: Tuesdays. Admission charge.*

### Webb-Deane-Stevens Museum

Three historic houses have been combined into a museum which gives a unique side-by-side comparison of the lifestyles of three very different people. All three houses have many original furnishings. *211 Main Street. Tel: (860) 529–0612. Open: May to October, Wednesday to Monday 10am–4pm, Sunday from 1pm; November to April, Saturday and Sunday 10am–4pm. Admission charge.*

Open for business in the Quiet Corner: one man's junk is another man's collectable

# Maine

*M*aine was the first part of New England to be discovered by Europeans. In the 11th century the Vikings sailed off these shores, but it was not until 1497 that the Venetian navigator John Cabot claimed the land (inhabited by several Algonquin tribes) for England. The French came in 1604 and, ignoring the English claim, Samuel de Champlain settled an island in the St Croix River. The long and bitter dispute between the British and French was not resolved until 1763. The protracted French and Indian War resulted in the loss of most of the land held by the French in North America.

Maine was part of Massachusetts for many years, but it seceded in 1819 and a year later became the 23rd state of the Union. It is as big as all the other New England states combined, and most of the area is covered in pine forests (hence its nickname, the Pine Tree State). But it is water for which the state is known. Although the coastline is only 230 miles as the crow flies, it is so rugged and indented that Maine has more lineal footage of coastline of any state in the Union – 3,500 miles. In addition, there are over 6,000 lakes and 32,000 miles of rivers.

Maine is a wet and wild state that is rightfully described as a vacation paradise (even car licence plates have 'Vacationland' emblazoned across them). Yet it has two distinctly different faces. Most holiday-makers are attracted to the coastline, that narrow strip along the Atlantic dotted with pictureque fishing villages, lighthouses and hidden harbours. During the summer, this corridor teems with thousands of people escaping from New York, and even Massachusetts, to enjoy this marine paradise.

The other Maine is a vast area of genuine wilderness with few towns and few people. The more remote parts of the state are virtually unexplored. Only the most fanatical fisherman, canoeist or hiker ventures into these areas and, of course, there is little in the way of accommodation or eating facilities for the casual visitor.

As in the rest of New England, autumn is a good time to visit. Not for the foliage, however – Maine does not have the same intensity of colour as the mountain states. But at this time of year, the heavy summer tourist traffic has left, children are back at school and Maine is back to its normal, tranquil self. Many of the attractions are only open during the summer, however, most close in the early autumn and reopen the following May. It is always advisable to telephone ahead to check opening times.

Autumn weather can be spectacular, with warm days and blue skies. Maine winters are often bleak, but there is some of the best skiing in the Northeast here. Spring can be superb, but swarms of black flies and mosquitoes are annoying.

Remember that Maine covers a large area. It takes several visits to see it properly, but for a taste of the state, a short visit to the southern part of the coast should be enough to whet most appetites for more. However, the further north you travel, the more unspoiled and picturesque it becomes.

# MAINE

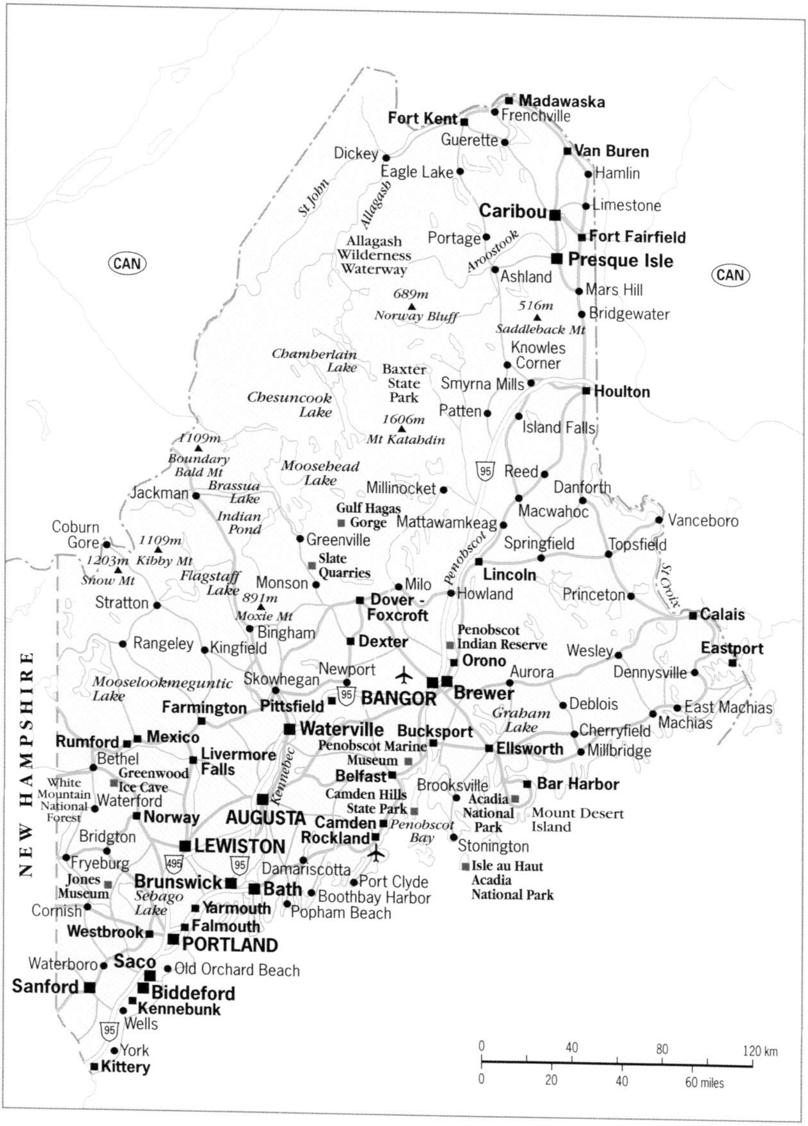

Madawaska
Frenchville
Fort Kent
Guerette
Dickey
Eagle Lake
Van Buren
Hamlin
St John
Allagash
Caribou
Limestone
Portage
Fort Fairfield
Allagash
Wilderness
Waterway
Aroostook
Presque Isle
Ashland
Mars Hill
CAN
CAN
689m
Norway Bluff
516m
Bridgewater
Saddleback Mt
Knowles
Corner
Chamberlain
Lake
Baxter
State
Park
Smyrna Mills
Houlton
Chesuncook
Lake
1606m
Mt Katahdin
Patten
Island Falls
1109m
Boundary
Bald Mt
Brassua
Lake
Moosehead
Lake
Millinocket
95
Reed
Danforth
Jackman
Indian
Pond
Gulf Hagas
Gorge
Mattawamkeag
Macwahoc
Vanceboro
Coburn
Gore
1109m
Greenville
Springfield
Topsfield
1203m Kibby Mt
Slate
Quarries
Penobscot
Snow Mt
Flagstaff
Lake
Monson
Milo
Lincoln
St Croix
891m
Stratton
Moxie Mt
Dover -
Foxcroft
Howland
Princeton
Calais
Rangeley
Kingfield
Bingham
Dexter
Penobscot
Indian Reserve
Wesley
Eastport
Mooselookmeguntic
Lake
Skowhegan
Newport
Orono
Aurora
Dennysville
Farmington
Pittsfield
95
BANGOR
Brewer
Deblois
East Machias
Rumford
Mexico
Waterville
Buckport
Graham
Lake
Machias
Bethel
Livermore
Falls
Penobscot Marine
Museum
Ellsworth
Cherryfield
Millbridge
White
Mountain
National
Forest
Greenwood
Ice Cave
Waterford
Belfast
Brooksville
Bar Harbor
Norway
AUGUSTA
Camden
Camden Hills
State Park
Acadia
National
Park
Mount Desert
Island
Bridgton
LEWISTON
Rockland
Penobscot
Bay
Stonington
Fryeburg
495
95
Damariscotta
Isle au Haut
Acadia
National Park
Jones
Museum
Sebago
Lake
Brunswick
Bath
Port Clyde
Boothbay Harbor
Cornish
Westbrook
Yarmouth
Popham Beach
Falmouth
PORTLAND
Waterboro
Saco
Old Orchard Beach
Sanford
Biddeford
Kennebunk
95
Wells
York
Kittery

NEW HAMPSHIRE

Kennebec

St John

Allagash

| 0 | 40 | 80 | 120 km |
| 0 | 20 | 40 | 60 miles |

## ACADIA NATIONAL PARK

The national park occupies most of Mount Desert Island, which was discovered in 1604 by Champlain. There are over 35,000 acres with 170 miles of hiking, biking and horse riding trails. Cadillac Mountain rises to 1,530 feet, the highest point on the eastern coast of the US. The Visitor Center (tel: 207 288–3338) shows a short film on the park and has free maps and guides. It also has a well-stocked bookstore for the naturalist and the weekly *Beaver Log*, listing the naturalist activities. Park Loop Road (see box) passes all the major sites and even goes to the summit of Cadillac Mountain. The road passes wild, rocky coastline, secluded sandy beaches and thick forests of conifers.

*Open: park accessible all year, but loop road closed in winter by snow. Visitor Center open: May to October 8am–6pm (or 4.30pm before 15 June and after 15 October). Admission charge.*

## AUGUSTA

Augusta, at the head of navigation on the Kennebec River, has been the state capital since 1832. Before then its main interest was commerce, particularly fur

In the vastness of Acadia National Park you can walk for miles without meeting others

and timber. The city began in 1628 as a fur trading post founded by members of the Plymouth Colony.

### Maine State Museum

This museum presents a fascinating and wide-ranging look at Maine's industries and natural environment with a historical perspective.

*State Street. Tel: (207) 287–2301. Open: Monday to Friday 9am–5pm, Saturday 10am–4pm, Sunday 1–4pm. Free.*

### State House

Designed by Boston's Charles Bulfinch and built of local granite, the building has been much extended; it has a graceful portico and many portraits and battle flags.

*State and Capitol Streets. Open: Monday to Friday 8am–4pm, tours from 9am. Free.*

## BANGOR

A commercial town 132 miles north of Portland (see page 110), Bangor is also known for hunting and fishing. Formerly the centre of the timber industry, catering to the basic needs of rough-and-tumble lumberjacks, it is Maine's most northerly town and has the definite feel of the frontier. Unless you are heading out into the wilderness on an adventure trip, there is not very much of interest here. The **University of Maine**, just north of Bangor, has a few museums, though not on a par with those of the Boston area.

*Chamber of Commerce, 519 Main Street. Tel: (207) 947–0307.*

## BAR HARBOR

Bar Harbor, at the entrance of Acadia National Park on Mount Desert Island, has several good shops and galleries and a very attractive harbour. It became a fashionable summer resort at the turn of the century for wealthy East Coast families like the Rockefellers, the Vanderbilts and the Pulitzers. At one time over 200 mansions overlooked the Atlantic. A disastrous fire in 1947 destroyed most of them; several of those that remain have been converted into inns. The **Bar Harbor Historical Society Museum** documents the town's dazzling past with photographs, newspapers and other memorabilia (34 Mount Desert Street – tel: 207 288–4245).

## BATH

Bath, 50 miles north of Portland, was a prosperous 19th-century seaport. The town's legacy is preserved in the **Maine Maritime Museum** (243 Washington Street – tel: 207 443–1316). In the **Percy and Small Shipyard** there is a collection of small wooden craft used on the coast of Maine in the last century. There is also an exhibit on early shipbuilding methods and workshops where apprentices are still learning these time-honoured crafts. From June to October, the *Sherman Zwicker*, a restored schooner, can be visited. *Museum, shipyard and schooner open: daily 9am–5pm. Admission charge.*

## BAXTER STATE PARK

The 200,000 acres of land for this park, 85 miles north of Bangor, were purchased by Percival Baxter – twice Governor – for the people of Maine. Baxter willed that this vast tract of prime forest near the Canadian border be maintained 'forever after in its natural, wild state'. The two highest mountains in the state are located here. Baxter Peak, the 5,267-foot summit of Mount Katahdin, is not only the highest point

Acadia's memorable sunsets fill the western sky with streaks of intense colour

in the state but also the end of the 2,000-mile-long Appalachian Trail, which starts in Georgia. This peak catches America's first rays of the sun each morning.

The park is not a place for the casual visitor. Although Route 159 passes through the park, most of the roads are unpaved and facilities are very basic. *Park Headquarters, 64 Balsam Drive, Millinocket. Tel: (207) 723–5140. Open: daily, mid-May to mid-October. Admission charge.*

The Loop Road on Mount Desert Island gives a 27-mile introduction to all the best sights in the park. For additional information write to the Superintendent, Acadia National Park, Box 177, Bar Harbor, Maine 04609.

## BOOTHBAY HARBOR

Lying 54 miles northeast of Portland, this town may appear to be the typical, picture-book fishing port for which Maine is famous, but beneath the surface is a full-blown tourist resort – complete with bowling alleys, pinball machines, silly hats and T-shirts. The summer crowds are proof of the town's appeal, but perhaps the best way to enjoy it is to take one of the many cruises, fishing trips and excursions on offer at the harbour (see **Monhegan Island**).

## BRUNSWICK

Education is one of the main pursuits of this town, located 25 miles northeast of Portland. Bowdoin College, founded in 1794, was the Alma Mater of Nathaniel Hawthorne, Henry Wadsworth Longfellow, explorers Robert Peary and Donald MacMillan, and US President Franklin Pierce. The husband of Harriet Beecher Stowe was a professor here when she wrote *Uncle Tom's Cabin.*

There are two museums attached to the college. The **Museum of Art** (Walker Art Building) has early American portraits and works by both Winslow Homer and Andrew Wyeth. More unusual is the **Peary-MacMillan Arctic Museum** (Hubbard Hall), which presents the history of polar exploration from ancient times to 1909, when Peary and his assistant MacMillan became the first to reach the North Pole.
*Bowdoin College, Main, Bath and College Streets. Tel: (207) 725–3000. Museums open: mid-June to August, Tuesday to Saturday 10am–5pm, Sunday 2–5pm; rest of year, Tuesday to Friday 10am–4pm. Free.*

## FREEPORT

Freeport, 17 miles northeast of Portland, is known as the home of L L Bean, the great American outdoor clothing and equipment supplier, open year round 24 hours a day. In recent years the town has become a centre for factory outlet stores. Many of the best-known labels and trade names have shops here, and their prices are far less than in their normal retail outlets.

## KENNEBUNKPORT

It was President George Bush who made Kennebunkport a household name. His spectacular home here, jutting out over the water, became the object of interest of people hoping to catch a glimpse of the First Family. Kennebunkport responded to the increased crowds with a beautification effort that has given the town an almost artificial air. Although undeniably attractive, with expensive boutiques, galleries and cute restaurants, there is a certain vapidity about the place.

The town, lying 26 miles south of Portland, is filled with historic 18th- and 19th-century homes, but virtually all are privately owned and not open to the public.
*Chamber of Commerce, 173 Port Road, Kennebunkport. Tel: (207) 967–0857.*

## MONHEGAN ISLAND

From Boothbay Harbor there is a boat trip that crosses the 10 miles of water to tiny Monhegan Island in 90 minutes. Locals are convinced that the Vikings landed here in the 11th century – which may or may not be true. In any case, the present small population of permanent residents make their living from fishing, lobstering and pleasure craft (see **Getting Away From it All**, page 147).

## PATTEN

See **Baxter State Park**, page 107.

Since the early 1900s yachtsmen and artists have been drawn to beautiful Boothbay Harbor

## PEMAQUID POINT

The coast of Maine has over 60 light-houses, but the Pemaquid Lighthouse, 31 miles southeast of Bath, is in one of the most dramatic situations, jutting out on rocky ledges carved by ancient glaciers. The lighthouse is open to the public and there are good views of the coast from the top. In the lighthouse keeper's cottage there is a small museum devoted to fishermen, with photographs and other artefacts related to their life. *Fishermen's Museum. Tel: (207) 677–2494. Open: daily 10am–5pm from Memorial Day to mid-October; rest of year by appointment. Donation.*

## PENOBSCOT BAY

The east corner of this huge, island-studded bay forms the western boundary of Acadia National Park. The waters are made for sailing. Tall-masted wind-jammers and schooners create images from another era as they gracefully navigate the islands.

On the western shore are Rockland, Rockport and Camden, incredibly picturesque fishing villages whose classic harbours overflow with sailing craft. They have mercifully escaped the ravages of tourist development and the only concession has been a proliferation of art and craft galleries and gift shops.

# PORTLAND

Although the biggest city in Maine, Portland is still an easy place to explore on foot and small enough to cover everything in a very short time. The town is often called 'the San Francisco of the East' – an exaggeration, perhaps, but it is nevertheless a town of considerable charm. Its hills sweep down to the harbour, and the general atmosphere is one of order and cleanliness. As most people visit Maine for the wild coast and romantic fishing villages, Portland has never suffered from tourist overcrowding or the garish attractions that usually sprout up where tourists congregate. It's a refreshing change to find a major town that is at once unspoiled and worth visiting.

The **Old Port Exchange** on the waterfront is a group of old warehouses that have been renovated and converted into shops, galleries and restaurants. It is a pleasant place to stroll and watch the activity of ferry boats and other maritime traffic around the wharfs.
*Chamber of Commerce, 60 Pearl Street. Tel: (207) 772–2811. Open: daily 9am–5pm.*

## Portland Museum of Art

This dramatic postmodern building, designed by the firm of I M Pei, houses a fine collection of work by notable Maine artists such as Andrew Wyeth, Winslow Homer and Edward Hopper.
*7 Congress Square. Tel: (207) 775–6148. Open: May to mid-October, Saturday to Wednesday 10am–5pm, Thursday and Friday 10am–9pm. Closed: Monday October to April. Admission charge.*

## Wadsworth-Longfellow House

The famous poet Henry Wadsworth Longfellow grew up in Portland, and his childhood home is now a museum. Built by his maternal grandfather, it was the first brick house in Portland.
*487 Congress Street. Tel: (207) 879–0427. Open: June to end-October, Tuesday to Sunday 10am–4pm. Admission charge.*

# SABBATHDAY

The **Sabbathday Shaker Community and Museum,** close to Sebago Lake, is one of the oldest Shaker settlements in the United States, established in 1782. The museum is comprised of a 1794 Meeting House, 1816 Spin House and 1839 Ministry Shop. The buildings have displays of simple but elegant Shaker furniture, textiles and farm tools.
*Route 66, New Gloucester. Tel: (207) 926–4597. Open: Memorial Day to mid-October 10am–4.30pm. Admission charge.*

# SEBAGO LAKE

Trout and land-locked salmon are Sebago Lake's big attraction for fishermen. All round the lakeshore there are resorts that cater for water sports enthusiasts of every kind. The crystal-clear waters are popular with both locals from Portland (20 miles to the south) and out-of-state visitors alike. At its north end, the lake – the second largest in Maine – has fine, sandy beaches that are ideal for swimming, but they can be overcrowded on summer weekends. Non-aquatic attractions around the lake include the Sabbathday Shaker Community and Museum (see above) and the **Jones Museum of Glass and Ceramics**, with over 7,000 items dating from ancient Egypt to the present day.
*Jones Museum, Douglas Hill. Tel: (207) 787–3370. Open: mid-May to mid-November, Monday to Saturday 10am–5pm, Sunday 1–5pm. Admission charge.*

## YORK

The southern coast of Maine, being within a 2-hour drive of Boston, is the most accessible to visitors. Many of the resorts are quite modern; the town of **Kittery**, just south of York, has developed as a centre for discount shopping. York, however, retains much of its old character. It is made up of three separate areas: York Village, York Harbor and York Beach. Apart from the beautiful beach and attractive harbour, there are several interesting historic sites in the town.

The **Old Gaol Museum** (York Street) opened in 1720 to serve all of Maine. The dark, dank cells are a harsh reminder of the severity of punishment for felons and debtors in the 1800s. The **Emerson-Wilcox House** (1742), has survived many transformations, from tavern to dwelling to tailor's shop to post office. Currently a museum, it has interesting period furnishings and costumed guides. Tours start at Jefferd's Tavern and Schoolhouse. A room above the bar was originally used by women and children and is now used as an orientation centre, with an exhibit of Maine's early school system.

*For information on the York Village historical complex, including tours, tel: (207) 363–4974. All the above are open mid-June to September, Tuesday to Saturday 10am–4pm. Admission charges.*

The limpid water of Sebago Lake invites swimming, boating, angling and more

# Rhode Island

*W*ith just over 1,200 square miles of land, Rhode Island (short for the State of Rhode Island and Providence Plantations) is the smallest state in the Union. It is divided into east and west by the deeply indented, island-studded Narragansett Bay, which provides some of the best sailing in New England. Altogether there are 400 miles of coastline in a state that is only 37 miles wide and it is virtually impossible to find any part of Rhode Island that is more than 25 miles from the sea. Not surprisingly for the undisputed sailing capital of the East Coast, Rhode Island's official nickname is 'The Ocean State'. All of the state's urban and industrial development lies to the east, with the rural areas to the west.

## NEWPORT

Most visitors to New England will find little time to explore the more esoteric neighbourhoods of Rhode Island, but this is one town that no visitor should miss. Like the state of Rhode Island, the town of Newport was settled by the same free thinkers who were fleeing from Puritan zealotry. By 1761 Newport was second only to Boston as a port involved in the infamous 'triangle trade', which traded molasses for slaves for rum. During the Revolution, the British occupied the town and virtually destroyed it. Newport never regained its commercial significance.

Wealthy planters from the Carolinas discovered Newport when trying to find relief from the heat and humidity of the South. Cool ocean breezes made this the perfect summer resort – and it is those same breezes that have made this the sailing capital of the coast.

The turn of the century was Newport's golden age, when the world's wealthiest families built summer 'cottages' overlooking the ocean that were the equal of the world's great stately homes (see pages 116–17).

Other events in recent years have consolidated Newport's position as an exclusive summer resort. John and Jackie Kennedy were married here, and their wedding reception was held at Hammersmith Farm near Fort Adams State Park. The America's Cup, the world's premier ocean-going yacht race, was held here for 50 years, and the world-renowned Newport Jazz Festival has been a magnet for fans every August for many years.

Today, Newport is a lively, attractive little town set dramatically against Narragansett Bay. Its main attraction is a collection of fabulous 'cottages' on Bellevue Avenue, which allow the visitor a glimpse of the lifestyles of yesterday's rich and famous. Eight of the most splendid mansions are maintained by the Preservation Society of Newport County (424 Bellevue Avenue – tel: 401 847–1000).

*Newport County Convention and Visitors Bureau, 23 America's Cup Avenue. Tel: (401) 849–8048.*

### The Astor's Beechwood

The tour here is pure theatre. Costumed actors and actresses play out the roles of servants, guests and hosts as they guide visitors both above

## RHODE ISLAND

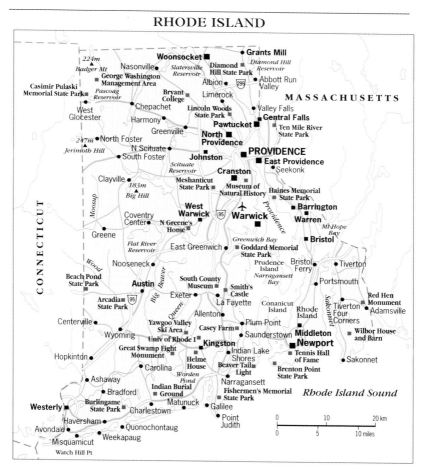

and below stairs.
*580 Bellevue Avenue. Tel: (401) 846–3772. Open: mid-May to October, daily 10am–5pm; November, daily 10am–4pm; February to mid-May, weekends 10am–4pm. Admission charge.*

**Belcourt Castle**
Designed in 1891 as the summer residence of Oliver Hazard Perry Belmont and his wife, this Louis XIII-style castle contains the country's largest collection of 13th-century stained glass and a golden coronation coach.
*Bellevue Avenue. Tel: (401) 846–0669. Open: February to March, November to December, daily 10am–3pm; April to October 10am–5pm. Admission charge.*

The Breakers, Newport's most splendid estate

## The Breakers
Built in 1895, the Breakers was modelled in the style of a four-storey Italian Renaissance villa. The 70 rooms are arranged round a great hall, and every surface is covered in polished stone and carved marble.
*Ochre Point Avenue. Tel: (401) 847–1000. Open: April to October, daily 10am–5pm (till 6pm Saturday, July to Labor Day). Admission charge.*

## Château-sur-Mer
Built for William Wetmore in 1852, this building represents one of the best examples of lavish Victorian architecture in the US.
*Bellevue Avenue. Tel: (401) 847–1000. Open: May to September, daily 10am–5pm, weekends only October and April; rest of year, weekends only 10am–4pm. Admission charge.*

## The Elms
This house was built in 1901, and was modelled on the Château d'Asnieres near Paris. The elegant landscaped grounds are a perfect complement to the splendour of the antique-filled rooms within.
*Bellevue Avenue. Tel: (401) 847–1000. Open: May to October, daily 10am–5pm; weekends only rest of year, 10am–4pm. Admission charge.*

## Hunter House
This is considered to be one of the best examples of Colonial architecture, open to the public, in America.
*54 Washington Street. Tel: (401) 847–1000. Open: May to September, daily 10am–5pm; weekends only in April and October. Admission charge.*

## Kingscote
Kingscote was built in 1839 by Richard Upjohn in a classic early Victorian style. Note particularly the Tiffany windows.
*Bellevue Avenue. Tel: (401) 847–1000. Open: May to September, daily 10am–5pm; weekends only in April and October. Admission charge.*

## Marble House
William Vanderbilt had this sumptuous mansion modelled after the Grand and Petit Trianons in Versailles. An authentic Chinese tea house sits at the end of a lawn overlooking the ocean.
*Bellevue Avenue. Tel: (401) 847–1000. Open: May to October, daily 10am–5pm; weekends only rest of year 10am–4pm. Admission charge.*

## Newport Casino
The Newport Casino (1880) was once a country club but is now home to the International Tennis Hall of Fame and the Tennis Museum. Here you can watch court tennis as it was played in the 15th century, and for a fee you can use the grass and indoor courts.
*194 Bellevue Avenue. Tel: (401) 849–3990. Open: year-round 10am–5pm. Admission charge.*

## Rosecliff
Yet another home modelled after a great French château. It was adapted by the architect Stanford White for Mrs

Hermann Oelrichs in 1902. The ball-room is the largest in Newport, and it was the scene of many memorable parties.
*Bellevue Avenue. Tel: (401) 847–1000.*
*Open: April to October, daily 10am–5pm.*
*Admission charge.*

### Touro Synagogue

This national historic site was the first Jewish place of worship in North America, built in 1763 and still in use today. The interior is considered an architectural masterpiece.
*85 Touro Street. Tel: (410) 847–4794.*
*Open: May to June, Monday to Thursday 1–3pm; late-June to Labor Day, Sunday to Thursday 10am–4pm, Friday 10am–3pm; September to October 15, Monday to Thursday 1–3pm. Free.*

### Wanton-Lyman-Hazard House

This is the oldest restored house in Newport. Built in 1675, it is a fine example of Jacobean architecture and has a restored Colonial garden.
*17 Broadway. Tel: (401) 846–0813.*
*Open: by appointment, summer hours. Call for times. Admission charge.*

### PROVIDENCE

The capital of Rhode Island is New England's third-biggest city. Providence does not have the attractions of Newport, but a pleasant hour or two can be spent visiting the more historic parts of town, such as Benefit Street, the State House and the area around Brown University.
*Greater Providence Convention and Visitors Bureau, 1 West Exchange Street. Tel: (401) 274–1636.*

### RISD Museum

The one site that merits greater attention is the RISD Museum, which is part of the Rhode Island School of Design. Don't be deceived by the rather ordinary look of the late Victorian building that houses this museum – inside are three floors of artistic treasures spanning several centuries.
*224 Benefit Street. Tel: (401) 454–6100.*
*Open: Wednesday to Sunday 10am–5pm, Friday 10am–8pm. Closed: New Year's Day, Easter, 4 July, Thanksgiving and Christmas Day. Admission charge (free on Saturday).*

Other places to visit include the **Roger Williams Park and Zoo**, 1000 Elmwood Avenue (tel: 401 941–3910); the **State House**, Smith Street (tel: 401 277–2311); the **John Brown House**, 52 Power Street (tel: 401 331–8575); and the **Providence Atheneum**, 251 Benefit Street (tel: 401 421–6970).

Fine views of Providence from Prospect Terrace, where the city's founder is buried

# Newport

This tour through Newport travels through 350 years of history, from pre-Revolutionary days when Newport was a major seaport rivalling Boston, Philadelphia and New York, highlighting its golden age of the late 1800s, when America's wealthiest families built their palatial 'summer cottages' overlooking the ocean. See pages 113–15 for fuller descriptions of some sites. *Allow 1½ hours, longer with visits.*

*Start at the corner of Long Wharf and Americas Cup Avenue. Follow Americas Cup Avenue to Memorial Boulevard and turn left into Spring Street. Continue to Touro Street and turn right.*

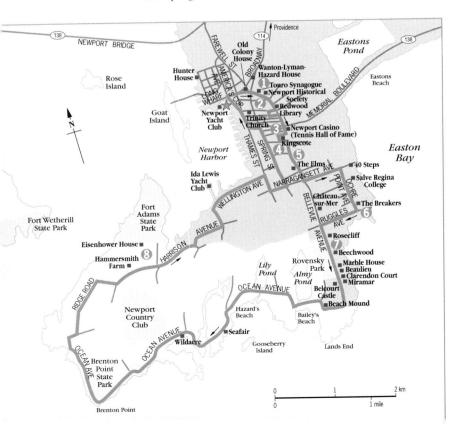

## 1 TOURO SYNAGOGUE

On the left is Touro Synagogue (see page 115).

## 2 NEWPORT HISTORICAL SOCIETY

Next to the synagogue is the Newport Historical Society. The building dates from 1729 and is the oldest Seventh Day Baptist Meeting House in America. In the museum there are displays of period furniture, paintings and rare books.
*Continue to Bellevue Avenue and turn right. Continue past Memorial Boulevard.*

## 3 NEWPORT CASINO

On the left is the casino (see page 114).
*Continue a short distance down Bellevue Avenue to Bowery Street.*

## 4 KINGSCOTE

Kingscote is on the right. This charming cottage was built in 1839 for George Noble Jones of Georgia and sold to China trader William King in 1864. It still contains the original King family furnishings (see page 114).
*Continue along Bellevue Avenue for one block past Perry Street.*

## 5 THE ELMS

On the right is The Elms, built in 1901 for coal magnate Edward Berwind.
*Continue and turn left into Narragansett Avenue, then right into Ochre Point Avenue.*

## 6 THE BREAKERS

The Breakers is on the left opposite Victoria Avenue (see page 114).
*Continue, turn right into Ruggles Avenue, then turn left to rejoin Bellevue Avenue.*

## 7 ROSECLIFF

Here, opposite Rovensky Park, is a remarkable concentration of great

An early haven for Quakers and Jews, Newport prospered in trade and shipbuilding

houses, starting with Rosecliff on the left and finishing with Belcourt Castle on the right. Beechwood, home of the Astors, is next door to Rosecliff, then Marble House, Beaulieu, Clarendon Court and Miramar follow (see pages 114–15).
*Follow Bellevue Avenue around until it becomes Ocean Avenue. Continue to Brenton Point State Park. Ocean Avenue eventually becomes Ridge Road.*

## 8 HAMMERSMITH FARM

On the left is Hammersmith Farm, the childhood summer home of Jackie Onassis. It was here that she and John Kennedy held their wedding reception in 1953. The 28-room mansion was used as Kennedy's 'summer White House'. Just behind Hammersmith Farm is President Eisenhower's summer White House, now used by the state for conferences and meetings.
*Ridge Road becomes Harrison Avenue. Continue and turn left into Wellington Avenue, then right into Thames Street, left into Narragansett Avenue and left into Spring Street. Follow Spring Street to Memorial Boulevard and turn left into Americas Cup Avenue.*

# New Hampshire

New Hampshire locals have a reputation for being independent and taciturn, characteristics inherited from their forefathers. It has become a popular place to live in recent years, particularly by commuters to Massachusetts, as it is the only New England state that has neither sales tax nor state income tax.

During the Revolution New Hampshire was the only New England state that was not invaded by the British, and it was the first to declare independence – seven months before the Declaration of Independence.

Between 1623 and 1653 settlements were established along the narrow, 18-mile corridor of coastline. Gradually the settlers moved inland, taming the wild landscape, which includes the highest mountains in New England. One of the beauties of this state is the variation of scenery in such a relatively small area – from windswept coast and mountains, to lakes or bucolic villages.

Today the state is a marriage of industry and wilderness. Manchester,

the largest town, has a strong 19th-century industrial atmosphere, with red-brick factories and warehouses. At the other extreme are remote hamlets north of the White Mountains that seem to belong in another century.

Apart from the Portsmouth area, it is the northern part of the state that offers the most interest to visitors. Natural beauty and grandeur are the attraction here rather than historic sites.

## CANTERBURY

Until very recently, two of the last surviving Shakers in New England lived here. The Shakers originally came over from Manchester, England, and established a settlement near Canterbury Center. As in other Shaker communities, they made their own furniture, tools and clothes; for things they could not produce, they traded medicines and herbs from their garden. The gardens are still planted with traditional plants, and herbs are on sale in the village shop. There are 22 buildings in the village, and several are open to the public. Craftsmen produce the simple and functional wares for which the Shakers were famous, such as brooms and nests of boxes. Canterbury is particularly unusual because of the restaurant serving traditional Shaker meals.
*Shaker Road, off Route 106. Tel: (603) 783–9511. Open: May to October, 10am–5pm. Closed: Sunday. Restaurant open: 11.30am–2.30pm. Admission charge.*

Canterbury's clapboard town hall

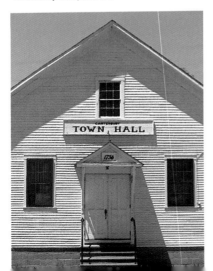

TOWN HALL

## NEW HAMPSHIRE

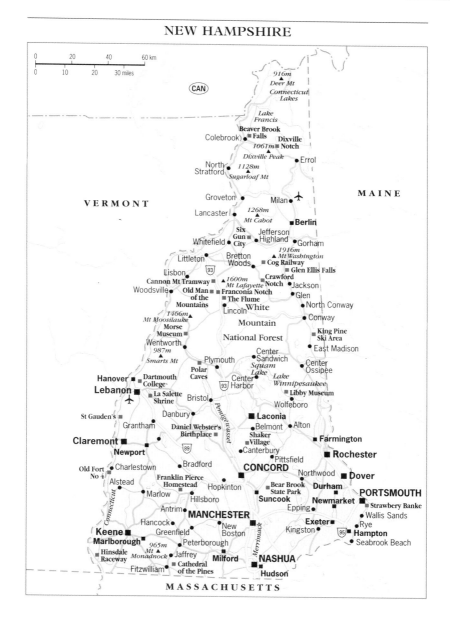

0  20  40  60 km
0  10  20  30 miles

**CAN**

916m
▲ Deer Mt
*Connecticut*
*Lakes*

*Lake*
*Francis*

**Beaver Brook**
Colebrook ● ■ **Falls**  **Dixville**
1061m ▲ **Notch**
*Dixville Peak*
North ● Errol
Stratford ● 1128m ▲
*Sugarloaf Mt*

**MAINE**

Groveton ●  Milan ● ✈
Lancaster ●  1268m ▲
*Mt Cabot*  **Berlin** ■

**VERMONT**

**Six**  Jefferson
**Gun**  Highland ●
Whitefield ● **City**  ● Gorham
1916m
Littleton ●  Bretton ● ▲ Mt Washington
Woods ■ **Cog Railway**
Lisbon ●  ■ **Glen Ellis Falls**
**Cannon Mt Tramway** ●  **Crawford**
▲1600m **Notch**
Woodsville ● **Old Man** ■ *Mt Lafayette* ● Jackson
**of the** ■ **Franconia Notch**
**Mountains** ■ **The Flume** ● Glen
1466m ▲  Lincoln ● **White** ● North Conway
*Mt Moosilauke* **Morse**  Conway ●
**Museum** ■ **Mountain**
Wentworth ●
987m ▲  **National Forest**
*Smarts Mt*  ■ **King Pine**
Center **Ski Area**
Polar ● **Sandwich** ● East Madison
**Caves** *Squam*  Center
Plymouth ● *Lake* Lake ● Ossipee
**Hanover** ■ ● **Dartmouth** Center *Winnipesaukee*
**Lebanon** ■ **College** ● Harbor ■ **Libby Museum**
● **La Salette** Bristol ●
**Shrine** Wolfeboro ●
**St Gauden's** ■  Danbury ● **Laconia** ■
Grantham ●  ● Belmont ● Alton
**Daniel Webster's**
**Claremont** ■ **Birthplace** ■ **Shaker** ● **Farmington**
**Newport** ■ **Village**
■ Canterbury ● **Rochester**
Old Fort ● Charlestown ● Bradford ● Pittsfield
No 4 ● **CONCORD** Northwood ● ● **Dover**
Alstead ● **Franklin Pierce**  **Bear Brook** **Durham** ●
**Homestead** ● Hopkinton ● **State Park**  **PORTSMOUTH**
Marlow ●  **Suncook** ● **Newmarket** ■ **Strawbery Banke**
Antrim ● Hillsboro ● Epping ● ● Wallis Sands
**MANCHESTER** **Exeter** ■
Hancock ● New ● Kingston ● Rye
**Keene** ■ Greenfield ● Boston ● ■ **Hampton**
**Marlborough** ■ 965m ▲ Peterborough ● ● Seabrook Beach
**Hinsdale** *Mt* ● **NASHUA**
**Raceway** *Monadnock* ● Jaffrey **Milford**
Fitzwilliam ● **Cathedral** **Hudson**
**of the Pines**

**MASSACHUSETTS**

## CONCORD

This has been the capital of New Hampshire since 1808. It is the home of the Concord coach, a high-wheeled wooden carriage that is credited with opening up the West. An example of the vehicle, used by Wells Fargo and other stage lines, can be seen at the **New Hampshire Historical Society and Museum**. The **Statehouse**, made of Vermont marble and local granite, is the only one in the nation where the legislature still meets in the original chambers.

*Concord Chamber of Commerce, 244 North Main Street, Carrigan Commons. Tel: (603) 224–2508.*

*Historical Society and Museum, 30 Park Street. Tel: (603) 225–3381. Open: daily 9am–4.30pm; Saturday and Sunday from noon. Donation.*

*Statehouse, Main Street. Tel: (603) 271–1110. Open: Monday to Friday 8am–4.30pm. Closed: holidays.*

## HANOVER

The Connecticut River Valley has many attractive towns, but none more so than Hanover. The town is synonymous with **Dartmouth College**; in fact, the Ivy League institution is so dominant that there would be no Hanover without it. Founded in 1755 by Eleazar Wheelock to spread Christian education among the Indians, the charity school moved to Hanover in 1769 and the name was changed to Dartmouth College. The campus is one of the most pleasant and beautiful imaginable. The college buildings are clustered around a beautiful Green that dominates the centre of Hanover. Particularly notable is Dartmouth Row, a group of four Greek Revival buildings that exude academic excellence. On the south side of the Green, the **Hood Museum of**

Dartmouth College has grown from a log hut to a campus boasting many handsome buildings

With its origins in logging and textile mills, Manchester has long been an industrial giant

**Art** houses 10 different galleries; exhibits range from Assyrian reliefs to Picassos. The other important works of art on the campus are frescoes by the Mexican muralist José Clemente Orozco in the **Baker Memorial Library** at the north end of the Green.

*Hanover Chamber of Commerce, 37 South Main Street. Tel: (603) 643-3115.*
*Baker Memorial Library. Tel: (603) 646-2560. Open: daily 8am–midnight; out of term, Monday to Friday 8am–8pm, Saturday 9am–6pm, Sunday 1–8pm. Free.*
*Hood Museum of Art, Wheelock Street. Tel: (603) 646-2808. Open: Tuesday to Saturday 10am–5pm, Wednesday until 9pm, Sunday noon–5pm. Closed most holidays. Free.*

## MANCHESTER

This town lies 20 miles north of the Massachusetts border on Route 3. Like its English namesake, Manchester has an air of industrialisation. In the 1800s the Amoskeag mills were the biggest textile factory in the world. The old mill building by the Merrimack River still dominates the town. Today Manchester is the biggest town in New Hampshire, with a population of over 100,000.

A site of general interest to visitors is the **Currier Gallery of Art**. The collection concentrates on European and American art from the 13th century to the present, and is considered one of the finest in the United States.

*Greater Manchester Chamber of Commerce, 889 Elm Street. Tel: (603) 666-6600.*
*Currier Gallery of Art, 192 Orange Street. Tel: (603) 669-6144. Open: Sunday to Thursday 11am–5pm, Friday until 9pm, Saturday 10am–5pm. Closed: Tuesday. Admission charge.*

## MONADNOCK

The southwestern corner of the state is much more mountainous than the southeast. Mount Monadnock, which rises to 3,165 feet, is climbed by more than 100,000 people each year. Deep in its valleys places like Fitzwilliam, Peterborough, Jaffrey and Keene have everything you associate with New England – white-steepled churches, quiet country roads and covered bridges.

The pride of a Portsmouth catch, with claws looking like a pair of boxing gloves

## PORTSMOUTH

New Hampshire's only seaport is not just the part of the state most accessible to Boston, but it is also one of the most interesting, with a wealth of historic sites dating back to 1630. This former state capital lies on the banks of the Piscataqua River. In the early 1800s the town was a thriving shipbuilding centre, and its sawmills provided masts and timber to British shipyards. With the decline of the wooden ship, commerce took over as the main focus of the local economy.

### Strawbery Banke

The first settlers in what is now called Portsmouth disembarked after their long sea journey to find the banks of the tidal inlet covered with wild strawberries. From such auspicious beginnings the waterfront settlement of Strawbery Banke developed into a prosperous seaport and centre of commerce. By the 1950s, however, the original historic area was in such a state of decay that it was threatened with 'urban renewal'. Concerned citizens saved it from such a fate by securing federal funds to restore the area. Thirty-eight buildings covering 10 acres were spared, and many of them have now been renovated and are open to the public. The restoration project has been done so well that it is hard to believe that Strawbery Banke was ever derelict.

Among the buildings of particular interest are the **First New Hampshire State House** (1758); the **Daniel Webster House**, home of the famous orator and statesman for two years; the **Captain Sherburne House** (1695); the **Captain John Wheelwright House** (1780), which is perhaps the finest Georgian building here; and the **Captain Keyran Walsh House** (1796), built on a triangular plot so that it has no right-angle corners. All the houses have period furnishings and are open to the public. The gardens of Strawbery Banke are filled with plants of the period, and craftsmen can be found throughout the site, not only using traditional methods in their restoration work but also making items for sale.

*Strawbery Banke Museum, enter off Marcy Street. Tel: (603) 433–1100. Open: May to October, daily 10am–5pm. Admission charge.*

Many other fine houses can be found close to Strawbery Banke, and the Greater Portsmouth Chamber of

Commerce (500 Market Street – tel: 603 436–1118) publishes the free *Portsmouth Trail*, a self-guided tour to eight historic homes. Most notable are the **John Paul Jones House**, which has the oldest piano in the United States on display, and the **Governor John Langdon House**, which George Washington visited in 1789.

Most of the houses close during the winter and at other times are only open a few days of the week. Always telephone ahead to confirm opening times.

## WHITE MOUNTAINS

The White Mountains are the highest range in New England. In the autumn the vibrant colours of the foliage up here are unsurpassable; in the winter, resorts like Loon Mountain attract skiers from all over the East Coast. The rest of the year it is simply a very beautiful place to be.

### Crawford Notch

A 'notch' in New Hampshire is a high mountain pass. This particular pass was discovered by a moose hunter in 1771, and four years later the first road was opened through it. The Crawfords were a family of pioneers in the White Mountains in the 19th century; they were responsible for cutting the first trail to the summit of Mount Washington. They had a cabin at the notch that was eventually named after them, and it often provided shelter to hikers.

On the west side of Route 302, driving down from Crawford Notch, a parking area marks the trail head for a one-hour hike to Arethusa Falls, which is the highest in the state.

Just north of Crawford Notch, there is one of the grand hotels of New

England, a lavish European-style spa. The **Mount Washington Hotel**, on Route 302 in Bretton Woods (tel: 603 278–1000), has been in operation since the 1800s. It was the site of a 1944 conference at which the United Nations established an international monetary programme and plans to establish the World Bank.

The **Mount Washington Cog Railway** departs from the Marshfield Base Station, about 6 miles east of Bretton Woods (see **Getting Away From it All**, page 142).

The John Paul Jones House, Portsmouth, where the Scots-born American Navy officer lived

**Franconia Notch**

Franconia Notch State Park is one of the great destinations of northern New England, and most of the sights can easily be seen along Route 93, the Franconia Notch Parkway. The park headquarters, at the north end of the Parkway, has maps and information on all park activities (tel: 603 823–5563).

Cannon Mountain is on the west side of the Parkway, and the **Cannon Mountain Aerial Tramway** provides a 5-minute gondola ride to the summit – a vertical ascent of over 2,000 feet – for spectacular views over three states and two countries. Cannon Mountain had the first engineered ski slopes in the United States. Appropriately, the **New England Ski Museum** is next door.

*Cannon Mountain Aerial Tramway, Franconia Notch Parkway. Tel: (603) 823–5563. Open: Memorial Day to Columbus Day, daily 9am–4.30pm. Admission charge.*
*New England Ski Museum. Tel: (603) 823–7177. Open: Memorial Day to third week of October, daily 10am–5pm. Free.*

The most famous landmark in the White Mountains can best be seen from the eastern shore of Profile Lake after 10am. **The Old Man of the Mountains** is a rock formation, high above the lake, that bears a striking resemblance to a man's profile (when P T Barnum saw it, he wanted to buy it for his circus!). The Old Man measures over 40 feet in length.

The **Basin**, a little further south on the Parkway on the west side, is a huge glacial pothole in the Pemigewasset River. South of this is **The Flume Visitor Center**, which has displays of historic photographs of the park and exhibits relating to the area's history.

This is also the entrance to **The Flume**, an 800-foot chute through which water plunges to the base of Mount Liberty. A series of stairways lead to the top of The Flume.

*The Flume, Franconia Notch Parkway. Tel: (603) 745–8391. Open: late May to late October, daily 9am–4pm. Admission charge.*

North of Franconia Notch is the village of Franconia. The **Frost Place** (off Route 116 – tel: 603 823–5510) is where the poet Robert Frost lived for several years. The simple wooden house is open to the public and contains Frost memorabilia. A Poetry Trail winding through the grounds inspired some of his best-loved poems.

*The Frost Place, off Route 116. Tel: (603) 823–5510. Open: weekends only Memorial Day to Labor Day, 1–5pm. Admission charge.*

Just along the road from Franconia is **Sugar Hill**. This quaint New England classic is spectacular in the autumn, when the maple leaves change colour.

**Kancamagus Highway**

The Kancamagus Highway, from Lincoln to Conway, is one of the great scenic drives in America. In the autumn it is unbeatable (see pages 128–9).

**Mount Washington**

Peaking at 6,288 feet, this is the highest mountain east of the Mississippi and north of the Carolinas. It is also one of the most dangerous. The highest wind speed ever recorded on earth was logged here at an astonishing 231mph. The wind-chill temperatures rival those of the polar regions.

In spite of the often harsh conditions, visitors have an insatiable desire to reach the top. Many go on foot, but a more

The Flume, a granite chasm where a mountain stream tumbles in a series of waterfalls

leisurely ascent can be made by rail. The scenic journey is a 3-hour round trip, in a smoky old steam train up seemingly impossible grades.

An alternative and cheaper, although less romantic, way to reach the top is by the Mount Washington Auto Road. There is a small museum with displays on the geology and wildlife of the area. Only experienced mountain drivers should attempt this road.

*Mount Washington Auto Road, off Route 16, near Gorham. Tel: (603) 466–2222. Open: daily mid-May to October (weather permitting); hours vary, phone for details. Admission charge. Museum open: Memorial Day to third week of October, daily 8am–8pm. Admission charge (nominal). Mount Washington Cog Railway, Route 302, Bretton Woods. Tel: (603) 846–5404. Open: mid-April to early November, daily (weather permitting). Admission charge.*

# LEAF PEEPING

**N**ew England is synonymous with spectacular autumn colour. Over 3 million visitors a year come to witness this unrivalled display of nature's beauty in a pastime known as leaf peeping.

The colour changes spread down from the far north, usually starting about the middle of September and peaking in the southern areas of the region by mid-October. The timing and degree of change depend upon the weather. A wet summer means a late season, while a dry, hot summer means the leaves will turn early.

The most dramatic colour occurs in the mountain areas of New Hampshire and Vermont (see pages 128–9). The White Mountains of New Hampshire are reputed to have some of the best fall foliage areas in the world, with over 750,000 acres of uninterrupted forests. The forested slopes of the White Mountains and Vermont's Green Mountains turn to shades of red, orange and yellow almost too bright and breathtaking to be believable.

For a classic New England fall, visit Vermont's Northeast Kingdom. Gentle, rolling hills covered in brilliant foliage are punctuated by white steepled churches, presenting the ultimate New England landscape. Every year in late September the week-long Northeast Kingdom Fall Foliage Festival is the biggest event in the region. Needless to say, accommodation for this period fills up several months in advance.

The White Mountains, the northern culmination of the Appalachian range, provide endless miles of dazzling autumn scenery, especially along the Kancamagus Highway

Events in Vermont are detailed in *Vermont Fall Events and Foliage Tours*, available from the Vermont Travel Division, 134 State Street, Montpelier, VT 05602, tel: (802) 828–3236.

Hotlines are provided by each state to give the latest information on leaf-peeping conditions.

| | |
|---|---|
| Connecticut | (203) 258–4290 |
| Maine | (207) 289–5710 |
| Massachusetts | (617) 727–3201 |
| New Hampshire | (800) 258–3608 |
| Rhode Island | (401) 277–2601 |
| Vermont | (802) 828–3239. |

Remember that this is the busiest season for visitors to New England – book well in advance.

# The Kancamagus Highway

The White Mountains of New Hampshire provide some of the most flamboyant autumn colours in the world. This northern section of the Appalachian Trail provides not only the most striking fall foliage but some of the most beautiful, unspoilt wilderness in all of New England. At any time of year, the Kancamagus Highway will inspire the traveller with its sweeping vistas. The highway connects the Pemigewasset River at Lincoln with the Saco River at Conway. Although the road was started in 1937, it was not until 1959 that the two halves were connected near the Kancamagus Pass. The highway is 34½ miles long and rises to almost 3,000 feet at its summit.

*Start in the tiny resort town of North Woodstock. There is an excellent visitor information centre here (tel: 603 745–8720), in addition to a wide range of accommodation and restaurants. The most notable sites along the Kancamagus Highway are mentioned here, but there are countless lookouts and picnic areas, each of which has its own special beauty. Drive east past Loon Mountain Ski Resort for about 11 miles.*

## 1  PEMI OVERLOOK

On the south side of the road, this dramatic overlook gives views of the mountains named after New Hampshire's most famous Indians: Passaconaway, Kancamagus, Paugus and

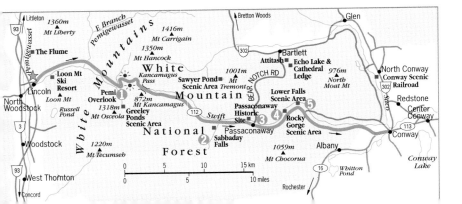

The highway is named for Indian chief Kancamagus, who strove for peace with the white man

Chocorua. Mount Kancamagus is the closest to the lookout, rising to 3,700 feet.

*Continue over the pass as the road follows the Swift River.*

## 2  SABBADAY FALLS

A five-minute walk along the Sabbaday Brook Trail ends at these falls, where the water pours from one huge pothole to another before rushing through a narrow flume.

*Continue for 1½ miles to a turn on the left.*

## 3  PASSACONAWAY HISTORIC SITE

A self-guiding trail follows the old railway and gives a good introduction to the trees and shrubs of the area. The site is an information and nature centre for White Mountain National Forest. During the summer there are demonstrations by craftworkers in period costume.

*Resume the drive along the highway.*

## 4  ROCKY GORGE SCENIC AREA

The river passes through a narrow canyon at this point, creating rapids that fall into a pond.

## 5  LOWER FALLS SCENIC AREA

The rapids are best viewed from the eastern end of the site. In the autumn these areas can be very crowded, and the best time to visit is midweek.

*The drive finishes in the small resort town of Conway.*

Passaconaway Historic Site. Open: end June to Columbus Day, daily 9am–5.30pm. Free.

# Vermont

*T*he 'Green Mountain State' is aptly nicknamed. Vermont is dotted with hamlets that are every American's dream of idyllic pastoral life. Quaint village greens, white steepled churches and sleepy country lanes combine with some of the most picturesque mountain scenery in North America to make this state a holiday paradise. In winter, the skiing is as good as anywhere on the East Coast, while in the autumn the forests are ablaze with colour. At any time of year you can savour the small-town atmosphere of a bygone era. Classic village stores are packed with wheels of cheese, jars of fresh maple syrup and hand-made ice cream; maple sugar houses steam away, producing the delectable amber syrup that Vermont is famous for, and traditional crafts-men still produce their wares using methods handed down for generations.

Vermont is a state to meander through. Travel slowly and let the countryside work its magic. Virtually every road offers scenery worthy of any calendar. Some of the most memorable and enjoyable experiences will be found by surprise – turning a bend in a country lane to find a picture-perfect village nestled in the woods, chatting with an old country store owner who has been in the same tiny village for 70 years. The pace of life here is slow – enjoy it.

After their first expedition here in 1609, the French controlled the area for nearly 150 years (the name of the state is derived from the French for green mountain). The British established their first settlement here in 1724 near Brattleboro, but it took another 35 years to defeat the French – and then the colony had to battle with New York over land claims. In 1770 Ethan Allen formed a local militia, the Green Mountain Boys, to protect the new settlers, and with the start of the American Revolution they joined other forces against Britain.

Vermont declared itself an independent state in 1777. It even had its own currency and postal service and established diplomatic relationships with foreign governments. After difficulties with New York were resolved, Vermont became the 14th state of the Union in 1791.

Vermont is the only New England state that does not have a coastline, but it is nevertheless bordered by water. Lake Champlain forms the boundary with New York on the west, and the Connecticut River with New Hampshire on the east. It is the second largest state in New England, but it has the smallest population. The biggest town – Burlington, on Lake Champlain – has a population of only 40,000.

For the outdoorsman Vermont has much to offer year round, from both downhill and cross-country skiing to fly-fishing. Trails through the Green Mountains are perfect for hiking, and the back roads could have been built for the bicycle. Added to these are windsurfing, canoeing, golf, tennis, even hot-air ballooning.

Vermont is not a state packed with specific sites that must be visited. It provides above all an opportunity to get away from it all, but there are a few places that should not be missed.

# VERMONT

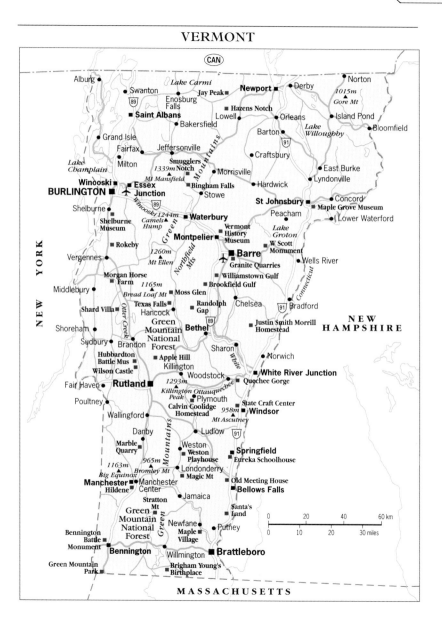

# STATES OF THE ARTS

New England has always been an inspiration to artists, and several painters and sculptors have made New England their home.

Many of the best-known artists of their time produced their major bodies of work in this historic corner of America. John Singleton Copley was the first major American portrait painter, closely followed by Gilbert Stuart, whose portraits of Washington are considered outstanding.

In more recent years, the great illustrator Norman Rockwell lived in Stockbridge, Massachusetts, from 1953 to 1978, producing over 300 covers for the weekly *Saturday Evening Post* magazine. His illustrations of ordinary American family life came to symbolise the vanishing values of another generation. Many of his former models still live around the Stockbridge area. The only collection of original art by Rockwell can be seen in the Norman

Rockwell Museum on Main Street.

In the last century Stockbridge was home to America's great monumental sculptor, Daniel Chester French. In his studio at Chesterwood, he produced the working models and plaster casts for the Abraham Lincoln statue that became his most famous work. Statues by the prolific French appear all over New England, including the Minuteman at Concord and the infamous John Harvard statue in Harvard Yard.

Just across the Massachusetts border lies the town of Bennington, Vermont. Anna Moses moved here after growing up a few miles away in New York State. At the age of 76 she took up painting and achieved international fame as one of the world's great primitives. Grandma Moses lived to be 101, dying in 1961 after 25 productive years. The Bennington Museum has a collection of her works, as well as her work table, on display in the

Opposite: brass sculpture of market debris set into the pavement of Boston's Blackstone Street.
Above: French's studio at Chesterwood.
Left: the Bennington Museum.
Below: the artist's distinctive signature on the museum sign

schoolhouse she attended in Eagle Bridge, New York.

In more recent years Andrew Wyeth has worked in Maine during the summer months, producing dramatic paintings of man's relationship to nature.

## BARRE

Pronounced *Bare-ee*, this is the home of the largest granite-producing quarries in the United States. In fact, the Rock of Ages Company has a quarry over 350 feet deep and covering 35 acres that is the biggest in the world. For over 150 years Barre granite has been used for the construction of public buildings, but now its major use is for headstones and memorials.

Four quarries in the area are still active, all of them operated by the Rock of Ages Company. They are actually in Graniteville, about 4 miles from the Barre Visitor Information Bureau. Adjacent is the Craftsman Center, where the rough granite is transformed into

Burlington, built on the terraced slopes of Lake Champlain, is the state's major city

finished sculpture and monuments.
*Rock of Ages, off Route 14, or off exit 6 of I–89. Tel: (802) 476–3115. Self-guiding quarry tours May to October, Monday to Friday 8.30am–5pm, Sunday noon–5pm; train tours 1 June to 15 October, Monday to Friday 9.30am–3.30pm. Admission charge. Craftsman Center open: Monday to Friday 8am–3.30pm. Free.*

Hope Cemetery to the north of Barre is an outdoor museum dedicated to the stonecarver's art. Headstones, many of them sculpted for the craftsmen's own families, represent the state of the art in monumental stonecarving. The cemetery is open from 7am to 4pm but closed every weekend.

## BENNINGTON

In both 1775 and 1777 Bennington was the centre of action during Revolutionary manoeuvres. The decisive Battle of Bennington is commemorated with a 306-foot-high limestone obelisk towering over the town. The observation platform at the top of the **Bennington Battle Monument** gives excellent views of the battlefield, town and neighbouring states. Back on the ground, a good place to start is the Bennington Area Chamber of Commerce (tel: 802 447–3311). The free walking tour maps will ensure that nothing is missed.

The **Old First Church** is one of the most photographed in New England. This Federal-style building, with its original box pews, has six columns, each made from a single pine tree. The cemetery beside the church contains the grave of Robert Frost; the epitaph, which he wrote himself, reads: 'I had a lover's quarrel with the world.' The **Bennington Museum** is most notable for its collection of the works of

Grandma Moses, the great American primitive painter. Her childhood schoolhouse was moved from Eagle Bridge, New York, and reconstructed as part of the museum. The rest of the museum houses Civil War and American Revolution artefacts, a collection of rare blown glass and a 3,000-volume genealogical library.
*Old First Church, 1 Monument Avenue. Tel: (802) 447–1223. Free.*
*Bennington Museum, West Main Street. Tel: (802) 447–1571. Open: daily November to May 9am–5pm; June to October 9am–6pm. Admission charge.*

## BRATTLEBORO
This was Vermont's first permanent settlement in 1724. It is now the most industrial town in the state, manufacturing paper, furniture products and leather goods, but it still retains its 19th-century atmosphere. The old granite Union Railroad Station houses the **Brattleboro Museum and Art Center**. Locally manufactured Estey organs were found in every household of prominence during the 1800s, and the museum has eight of these wooden organs on display.
*Brattleboro Chamber of Commerce, 180 Main Street. Tel: (802) 254–4565.*
*Brattleboro Museum and Art Center, Main and Vernon Streets. Tel: (802) 257–0124. Open: May to October, Tuesday to Sunday noon–6pm.*

## BURLINGTON
Vermont's biggest town is situated on the shore of Lake Champlain, which, after the Great Lakes, is the largest lake in the United States. It is 150 miles long, and has become an important recreation and holiday resource.

Sightseeing cruises last from 90

Lake Champlain's Discovery Festival includes a fishing derby, jazz festival and food fair

minutes to six days, and there are also regular ferry crossings to New York State, on the western shore of the lake (for ferry information, tel: 802 864–9804).

Burlington has long been an academic centre. The **University of Vermont** was established here in 1791 and sits above the town overlooking Lake Champlain from behind green lawns. There is a fine collection of primitive art in the university's **Robert Hull Fleming Museum** on Colchester Avenue (tel: 802 656–0750).

High-tech industries have been introduced, revitalising the industrial base on which the town was founded.
*Lake Champlain Regional Chamber of Commerce, 209 Battery Street. Tel: (802) 863–3489.*

Montpelier's colonnaded court house symbolises the ideal of democratic justice

## JAY PEAK

Almost at the Canadian border, Jay Peak Ski Resort gets an average of 300 inches of snow a year. Both downhill and cross-country enthusiasts are catered for, but even non-skiers will enjoy a ride on the aerial tramway to the 4,000-foot summit, where there are superlative views of the White Mountains, Lake Champlain, the Adirondacks and into Canada.
*Tramway open: late June to mid-October, daily 10.30am–4.30pm. Admission charge.*

## MANCHESTER

For more than 100 years Manchester has been a fashionable resort town. Its elite Equinox House Hotel was once frequented by Presidents Taft, Grant and Theodore Roosevelt. Tree-lined, marble pavements surround the Equinox House Historic District. Close to Manchester Center are the ski resorts of Stratton, Bromley and Magic Mountain.

### American Museum of Fly Fishing

One of America's oldest and most famous fishing tackle manufacturers, Orvis, is based in Manchester, and this museum is close by. Displays of over 3,000 flies and 1,000 rods trace the history of the sport. There are also displays of the tackle belonging to Ernest Hemingway, Dwight Eisenhower, Bing Crosby and other celebrities.
*Route 7A, Manchester Village. Tel: (802) 362–3300. Open: daily 10am–4pm. Closed: Christmas, New Year's Day and Thanksgiving. Admission charge.*

## Hildene

The former home of Abraham Lincoln's son Robert sits in 412 beautifully landscaped acres 2 miles south of town. The 24-room Gothic Revival mansion was built in 1905 as a summer home for Lincoln, who at the time was chairman of the Pullman Car Company. The house is now a museum full of period furnishings and Lincoln memorabilia.
*Route 7A, Manchester Village. Tel: (802) 362–1788. Open: mid-May to October, daily 9.30am–4pm. Admission charge.*

## MONTPELIER

The state capital is dominated by the gleaming, golden dome of the State House, which was modelled after the Temple of Theseus in Greece. Although this is a very pleasant city cradled in wooded hillsides, there is not very much of interest to the visitor.
*Vermont Travel Department, 134 State Street. Tel: (802) 828–3236.*

## NORTHEAST KINGDOM

For lovers of peace, solitude and wide open spaces, this is the area to visit. **St Johnsbury** is the industrial, retail and cultural centre of the region, and the town depends heavily on the maple syrup industry and trucking. The **Maple Grove Museum**, with a candy factory and sugaring house, gives a good introduction to the production of maple syrup. However, up here in the far north it is the tiny hamlets and rolling hillsides that are of more interest. Mile upon mile of forests, lakes and valleys are punctuated by the occasional storybook village. Hours can pass without seeing any other person – except during the autumn. When the leaves turn, the Northeast Kingdom Annual Foliage Festival offers flea markets, pancake breakfasts, harvest festivals and other events, usually at the end of September or beginning of October.

*Details can be obtained from the St Johnsbury Chamber of Commerce (tel: 802 748–3678).*

## PEACHAM

Peacham (21 miles southwest of St Johnsbury, on Route 15) is perhaps the most picturesque of the Northeast Kingdom villages, with its white houses, steepled church and splendid academy. It is certainly the most photographed during the foliage season, but should not be missed at any time of year. A classic general store has just about everything that the population of 611 could need.

## PLYMOUTH

Plymouth (6 miles south of Route 4 on Route 100) was the birthplace of Calvin Coolidge, the 30th President of the United States. Upon the death of President Warren Harding, Coolidge (Harding's Vice President) was sworn into office here by his father, a notary public. The **Coolidge Homestead** and **Coolidge Birthplace** are open to the public. He is buried nearby.

## QUECHEE GORGE

Not far from Woodstock, Route 4 crosses a high bridge. Stop, walk and look over the edge into a rocky chasm of immense proportions, carved out by the Ottauquechee River during the Ice Age. It is a 1-mile walk to the bottom of the 165-foot-deep gorge, known as 'Vermont's Little Grand Canyon'.

In Peacham, a family of scarecrows dressed in their Sunday best and ready to go

## RUTLAND

Vermont's second-largest town was the hub of the state's railway industry in the 1800s. It was also an important centre for quarrying marble: 250,000 headstones at Arlington National Cemetery in Virginia came from here, as did the marble for the Lincoln Memorial in Washington. The **Vermont Marble Company Exhibit** (61 Main Street – tel: 802 459–3311) explains the history of the industry with a series of descriptive displays.

Ten miles to the east is the top winter sports resort of **Killington**.

## SHELBURNE

One of the biggest man-made attractions in the state is the **Shelburne Museum**, with 37 buildings covering 45 acres. Apart from paintings and other fine art, there are numerous esoteric collections: a wildfowl decoy museum, a museum of hats and fragrance, a 892-ton sidewheel steamship, a 500-foot miniature circus parade, a 1786 sawmill, a 1783 stagecoach inn filled with American folk sculpture – in short, three centuries of Americana.

*Tel: (802) 985–3346. Open: mid-May to October, 10am–5pm. Admission charge.*

**Shelburne Farms** was part of the estate of Dr William Seward Webb and his wife, Lila Vanderbilt Webb. It is still in operation as a learning centre, and includes a working dairy farm and a cheese factory. The 110-room Queen Anne Revival house operates as an inn. Covered-wagon tours of the 1,000-acre estate and other events are offered throughout the summer.

*Tel: (802) 985–8686. Open: mid-May to mid-September, 9am–5pm. Admission charge.*

## STOWE

Stowe, with over 60 miles of cross-country ski trails, was the home of the famous Von Trapp family immortalised by *The Sound of Music*; the countryside reminded them of their native Austria. The **Trapp Family Lodge**, on Route 108, is a year-round resort.

## WOODSTOCK

This elegant town of well-preserved Federal-style houses has a large village green, an old covered bridge and four church bells that were made by Paul Revere. On the corner of Central and Elm streets, a bulletin board publicises local events.

The **Billings Farm and Museum** is a working dairy farm with a museum showing life on an 1890s farm. Frederick Billings, father-in-law of John D Rockefeller, made his money in railroads, but his interest was in animal husbandry and conservation.

*Tel: (802) 457–2355. Open: May to October, 10am–5pm. Admission charge.*

Self-expression in the resort of Woodstock

# GETTING AWAY FROM IT ALL

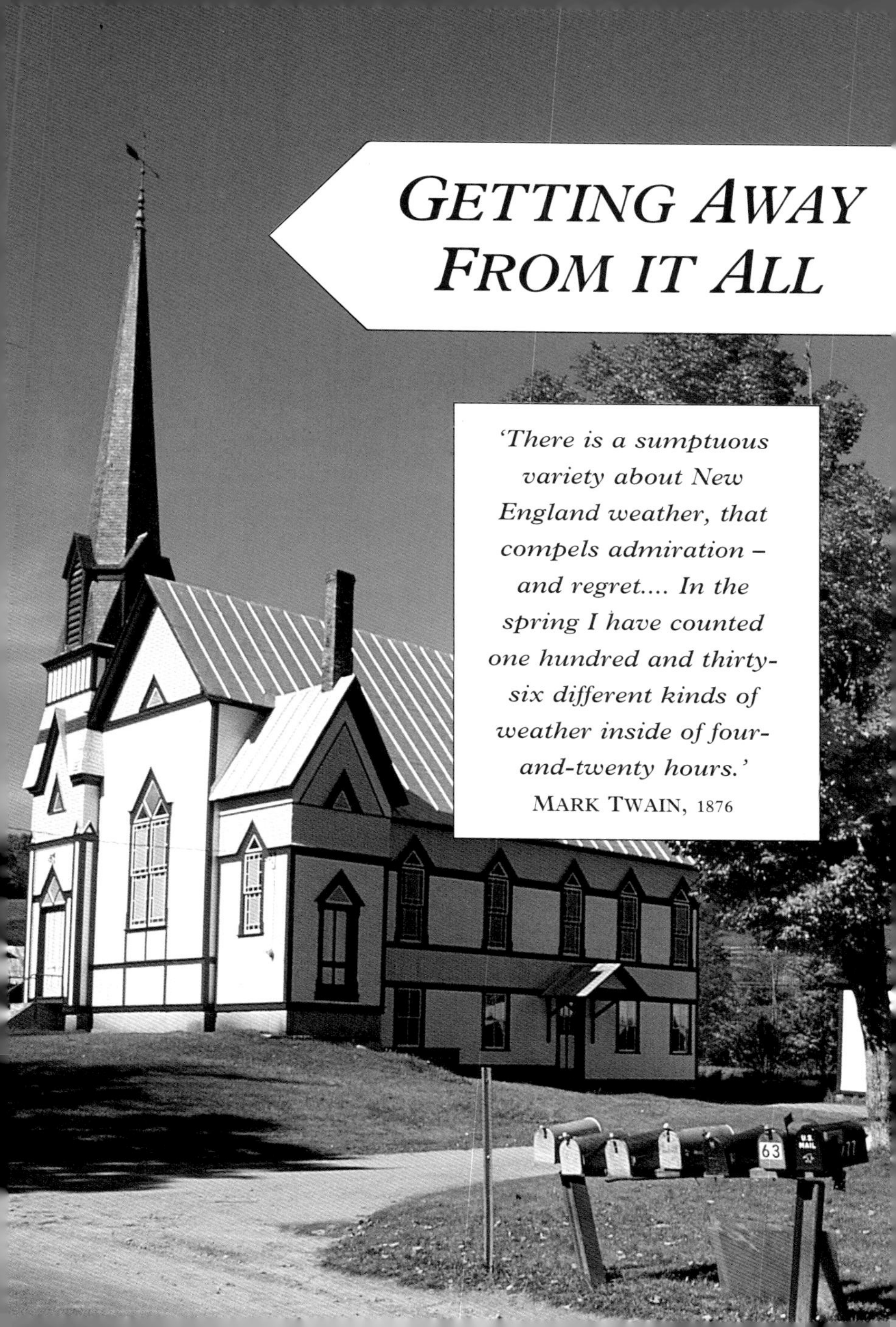

'There is a sumptuous variety about New England weather, that compels admiration – and regret.... In the spring I have counted one hundred and thirty-six different kinds of weather inside of four-and-twenty hours.'

MARK TWAIN, 1876

# Getting Away From it All

## SYLVAN SOLITUDE

Thirty minutes from downtown Boston, on Jamaica Plain, there are over 7,000 different species of trees and shrubs and hardly any people. The **Arnold Arboretum** of Harvard University started as a tree farm in 1872, and now plants and trees from around the world fill its 265 acres. The park is particularly spectacular during May and June, when many of the specimens are in full bloom. There are a number of paths through the arboretum, offering walks of up to an hour in length.

*125 Arborway, Jamaica Plain. Tel: (617) 524–1718. Open: daily from sunrise to sunset. Free.*

## A GRAVE AFFAIR

When **Mount Auburn Cemetery** was opened in Cambridge in 1831 it caused a sensation. As the first cemetery in the United States to be landscaped, it changed the way cemeteries were to look from then on. Many older cemeteries were cleaned up and the headstones rearranged for appearance, rather than in relationship to the bodies below!

This 170-acre botanical garden, complete with lakes and bridges, is also the resting place for many of Cambridge's and Boston's most notable figures. Henry Wadsworth Longfellow lies here, along with jurist Oliver Wendell Holmes, architect Charles Bulfinch, suffragist Julia Ward Howe, and Mary Baker Eddy, the founder of the Christian Science Church.

*580 Mount Auburn Street, Cambridge. Tel: (617) 547–7105. Open: daily until dusk.*

Humpback whale off the Massachusetts coast

## BLUE HILLS RESERVATION

This 6,500-acre park south of Boston is a vast recreational playground below the highest point in eastern Massachusetts. The Great Blue Hill is the site of the oldest weather station in North America, and a lookout gives tremendous views of the city of Boston to the north. There are dozens of hills covered with forest, and sheltering lakes filled with trout, bass, bullhead, perch and sunfish. There are over 500 miles of hiking trails and, in the winter, cross-country ski trails. Bridle trails for horses and biking trails are also provided. Other facilities include ice-skating rinks, tennis courts, a golf course, picnic areas and even a downhill ski run. The **Trailside Museum** is a natural history museum with live animals, and the 1795 **Redman Farmhouse** is among 16 historic sites.
*Reservation Headquarters, 695 Hillside Street, Milton. Tel: (617) 698–1802. Open: Tuesday to Sunday, but car parks open daily from dawn to dusk. Free. Trailside Museum. Tel: (617) 333–0690. Open: Wednesday to Sunday 10am–5pm, also Monday during holidays. Admission charge.*

## WET AND WILD

**Belle Isle Marsh** is the last extensive area of saltmarsh remaining in the city of Boston. In the 1630s it was grazing land for sheep, but now it is wild marsh set off by the unusual backdrop of the Boston skyline. There are walkways throughout the marsh; don't be surprised if you are the only person exploring them.
*To get there, take the T to Suffolk Downs Station.*

## WATCHING WHALES

Whales cruise off the New England coast from April to November, gathering at the major feeding grounds off the

Mount Auburn Cemetery: memorial to Mary Baker Eddy, founder of Christian Science Church

Massachusetts coast, Jeffery's Ledge and the Stellwagen Bank. These huge mammals reach up to 70 feet in length; among the species that can be seen are the finback, the humpback, minkes and right whales.

Gloucester claims to be closest to the feeding grounds, but whale-watching cruises operate out of most of the major seaports, including Provincetown on Cape Cod and Portsmouth, New Hampshire.

In Boston, cruises are operated by several companies including: **New England Aquarium** (tel: 617 261–6633), **AC Cruise Lines** (tel: 617 425–8419) and **Bay State Provincetown Cruise** (tel: 617 748–1428).

Seats are limited on the Cog Railway, so advance ticket purchase is recommended

## LETTING OFF STEAM

Steam engines are alive and well in New England. The world's first mountain-climbing locomotive was 'Old Pepperass', which reached the summit of Mount Washington on 3 July 1869. The engine is now on display at the base station for New Hampshire's **Mount Washington Cog Railway**, which is still the only cog railway in the world entirely powered by steam. It takes 2 tons of coal and 2,000 gallons of water to push one carriage to the top of the mountain. The 3-mile journey, which takes 3 hours, is the second-steepest railway track in the world. The train operates from early May to early November, depending upon the weather (see page 123).
*Route 302, Bretton Woods, NH. Tel: (603) 846–5404.*

Down on the Mount Washington Valley floor, the **Conway Scenic Railroad** takes passengers on a journey back in time in both open and closed restored carriages. The one-hour ride covers 11 miles and finishes at the 1874 depot, which has a small museum. A dining car has recently been added to the train to make the ride even more enjoyable.
*Route 16, North Conway, NH. Tel: (603) 356–5251. Open: mid-April to Christmas.*

In Connecticut, the **Valley Railroad** winds for an hour up the beautiful Connecticut River Valley from Essex to Chester using a 1920s steam engine and rolling stock. A delightful variation on the trip is to disembark at Deep River and take a leisurely riverboat journey back to Essex (see page 98).

Railroad Avenue, Essex. Tel: (203) 767–0103. Open: May to December. Telephone for times.

The **Berkshire Scenic Railway** in Lenox, Massachusetts, runs only diesel engines, but the ride will delight any railway enthusiast. As the railway is run by volunteers on a very irregular basis, it is always essential to telephone for schedules. There is an interesting collection of memorabilia at the Lenox depot.
*Housatonic Street, off Route 7 (Lenox Bypass). Tel: (413) 637–2210.*

## LOOKING AT LAKES

**Lake Winnipesaukee,** covering 72 square miles, is the largest lake in New Hampshire. It is surrounded by three mountain ranges and has 365 islands. The Indians called it 'the beautiful water in a high place', and the best way to experience it is aboard the MS *Mount Washington.* During the summer this 230-foot passenger steamship gives daily 50-mile, 3¼-hour cruises of the lake as well as evening theme cruises; every Sunday during the season there is a champagne brunch cruise.
*Departs from Weirs Beach daily from May to October. Tel: (603) 366–2628.*

A more original way to see the area is aboard the MV *Sophie C* mail boat, which delivers the post to summer residents of the islands in the northern part of the lake. This is the country's first floating post office, established in 1892.

Ideal for seeing the countryside

*Departs from Weirs Beach daily in May, June and September at 1.30pm; during July and August, daily at 11am and 1.30pm.*

On **Lake Champlain** in Vermont, throughout the summer, there are several daily ferries that make the one-hour crossing from Burlington to Port Kent in New York, providing an inexpensive way to enjoy the scenery.

Skipper of the *Mount Washington*: the original side-wheeler of that name was built in 1872

# 'THAR SHE BLOWS'

'Thar she blows!' – that familiar refrain shouted from the crow's nest of a ship by a sailor on watch – was the call to action for whaling, one of 19th-century New England's most important industries. Referring to the misty spray a whale emits when surfacing to breathe, the sailor's cry signalled an era of prosperity for New England that lasted for more than a century.

Captured in Herman Melville's novel *Moby Dick*, whaling was a hard life that carried great risks – and riches. Whale oil was used to light streets and homes in the United States and Europe during much of the 18th and 19th centuries. The main suppliers were the hundreds of ships based in Nantucket and New Bedford that scoured the oceans from Greenland to Polynesia.

Three-masted whale ships carried a crew of 15 to 20 on trips that kept men on the open waters for months at a time. The hunt began when harpooners on small rowing boats would hurl their weapons at an area just behind the animal's eye. Harpooned whales would then either dive, attack the boat or flee, pulling the boat along in what was known as a 'Nantucket sleigh ride'. Eventually, the whale would succumb to a series of carefully placed spears, and the processing of whale oil, meat and other whale products would begin on board the ship.

With the discovery of petroleum in 1859, whaling began a precipitous decline. Today whaling is banned in the United States, yet the cry of 'thar she blows' can still be heard aboard ships that take adventurous visitors on whale-watching trips from early summer to late October. In Provincetown try

Above: the tail fluke of each humpback whale is uniquely marked and helps identify individual whales who return to feeding grounds like the Stellwagen Bank year after year. Above right: close encounter with a giant; humpbacks can reach 40 to 50 feet and weigh 30 tons. Right: a Nantucket sleigh ride

Dolphin Fleet (tel: 508 255–3857) or Whale Watcher (tel: 508 362–6088); several other companies also offer trips along the North Shore of Massachusetts and the Maine coast.

## ISLAND HOPPING

The coast of New England is scattered with islands. Some are major resorts like Martha's Vineyard, while many are just rocks sticking out of the sea. But there are a few that allow the ideal escape away from the crowds.

In Boston Harbor there are over 30 islands. Some have been joined to the mainland, one group became Logan Airport, and several were used for housing prisoners or soldiers for strategic purposes.

**Georges Island** is the site of Fort Warren, built in the mid-1800s. It was used as a prison for Confederate soldiers during the Civil War, and since then it has been left more or less undisturbed. It is also the headquarters for the **Boston Harbor Islands State Park**, which covers seven islands in the bay. The ferry

Small ferries link many of the islands. This one is at Martha's Vineyard

to Georges Island from Long Wharf in Boston takes about 45 minutes.

During the summer, free water taxis serve **Gallops, Lovells, Peddocks, Bumpkin** and **Grape Islands**. On **Little Brewster**, the most remote island, stands the Boston Light, the oldest lighthouse in the country and the only one still manned by keepers. The original lighthouse, built in 1716, was blown up by the British in 1776; the present building was constructed in 1782.

All of the islands give great views of the Boston skyline, and some of them have primitive camping facilities.

Several organisations operate boat services to the islands: **Friends of Boston Harbor Islands** (tel: 617 523–8386) offers cruises to the more remote islands; **Boston Harbor Cruises** (tel: 617 227–4321); **Boston Harbor Commuter** (tel: 617 740–1253); and **Bay State Provincetown Cruises** (tel: 617 723–7800).

Waterfront homes and the harbour on Nantucket Island

## Block Island

Lying 12 miles south of Newport, Block Island is Rhode Island's answer to Nantucket and Martha's Vineyard – without the glitter. Several ferries operate daily from Point Judith, and the crossing takes an hour. During the summer there are also ferries from Providence, Newport, New London, Connecticut, and Montauk, Long Island. All the ferries usually have space available unless you are travelling with a car. Block Island is only 7 miles long and 3 miles wide and ideally suited to discovery by hired bicycle or moped. Mopeds are restricted on some of the smaller dirt roads, so bicycles are really the best way to travel around.

The island is relatively undeveloped and facilities are deliberately limited. During the summer, accommodation is booked solid for months ahead, so plans must be made well in advance.

Old Harbor is the first settlement you see on the island. A tourist boom early this century resulted in a number of grand hotels and restaurants being built

there, and these still stand to greet visitors from the mainland. From here a good paved road circles the island, leading to many pristine beaches and natural history trails. The interior of the island is grassy moorland. South of Old Harbor is the Southeast Point Light, close to the spectacular, multicoloured, 200-foot cliffs of Mohegan Bluffs. At the northern end of the island is a bird and wildlife refuge called Sandy Point.

There is a profusion of islands off the coast of Maine, but **Monhegan Island** is a perennial favourite. The ferry to the island, a mail boat called *Laura B*, leaves from Port Clyde, 9 miles away on the mid-Maine coast (twice daily during summer, reservations essential). The short crossing transports visitors to another century. Monhegan Island was settled in 1720 and has not changed much since then. There is still no electricity and few vehicles. Lobster-fishing is the only industry on the island, although a small artists' community has been attracted by the location.

## SALTWATER SAILING

Newport has long been considered America's sailing capital, so where better could one to learn to sail? The **Offshore Sailing School** offers courses with 20 hours of instruction, starting on Sunday evenings and running until Thursday. Its two courses – Learn to Sail and Bareboat Cruising Preparation – are conducted aboard a 27-foot Olympic-class Solings and a 36-foot Hunter, with no more than four students assigned to a boat. The school was founded by Olympic sailor Steve Colgate in 1964 and has taught over 75,000 people to master the waves.

*For information contact the head office of Offshore Sailing School at 16731 McGregor Boulevard, Fort Myers, Florida 33908. Tel: (800) 221–4326 (toll-free).*

## SPORTING OPPORTUNITIES

### Cycling

With its winding roads, irregular terrain and scenic small towns, New England

Cycling in New Hampshire's White Mountains

has drawn bicycle-touring enthusiasts from across America and around the world. In Boston, peddle on the Dr Paul Dudley White Bike Path, a 25-mile loop that takes you from the Science Park to Watertown Square along the historic Charles River. Visitors to Vermont can enjoy wonderful tours of country towns on their own or with **Vermont Bicycle Touring** (tel: 808 453–4811), one of several cycling companies that offer weekend or longer tours in the region.

### Hiking

The Appalachian Trail, one of the best-maintained hiking routes in America, runs the length of New England, up pristine mountain ridges and through lush valleys. The 5-mile hike up the region's tallest peak, 6,288-foot Mount Washington in New Hampshire, gives a sense of the diversity of New England flora and fauna. The trek takes you from deciduous forest to Arctic tundra, the botanical equivalent of travelling 600 miles north to the Canadian wilderness. The **Appalachian Mountain Club** (tel: 603 466–2727) maintains trails and a string of huts along the trail and can offer assistance in planning a trip or reserving a hut.

### Canoeing/kayaking

The Appalachian Mountain Club also provides information on navigating New England's inland waters. Dotted with freshwater lakes and rivers – from Lake Winnipesaukee in New Hampshire to the Saco River in Maine – the six-state region can keep paddlers pushing hard for weeks. There is great appeal in canoeing from inn to inn.

For details of other sports, see pages 162–5.

BULL&FINCH

PUB

'I like them all (New Englanders) extremely well,
but I do not wish to have any business transactions with
them, if I can avoid it, lest to use their
own phrase, "they should be too smart for me."'
MRS FRANCES TROLLOPE, 1832

# Shopping

New England is a shopper's dream. Not only can you find anything and everything, but the prices are attractive too.

## BOOKS AND MUSIC

Discounting books has become an accepted practice in the US, and many newly published works are available at substantial discounts. **Barnes and Noble** is one of the biggest quality discount chains. Both Boston and Cambridge have an abundance of outstanding bookshops catering to every interest.

LPs are now virtually unobtainable, but for cassettes and compact discs **Tower Records** and **The Wherehouse** have the greatest selection and the best prices.

## CLOTHES

Clothes are available in a wide variety of styles and prices, from French designer dresses and Saville Row suits to denim jeans. For the height of fashion and designs from the couture houses, there is no shortage of shops. Boston's Newbury Street is full of them – but don't expect a bargain. But there are some great buys to be found, if you know where to look.

For casual and work clothes, department store chains **J C Penny** and **Montgomery Ward** are hard to beat. At the other end of the spectrum are **Nieman Marcus**, **Nordstrom** and **Sak's Fifth Avenue**, which have designer clothes and recognised name brands. Frequent sales offering good savings are always well-advertised in local newspapers.

Provisions in The Dock at Lake Sunapee, NH

The best buys in New England are to be found in the basement of **Filene's**, a department store in Boston's Downtown Crossing. It is full of incredible bargains from major manufacturers, including designer labels. Each week the garments are increasingly discounted until sold. The prices are often as low as 10 per cent of the original price.

Outlet stores, operated by manufacturers, feature seconds and discontinued lines at very low prices. Some of the best, including **Ralph Lauren's Polo** shop and **L L Bean** (a mail-order outdoor clothing and equipment supplier), are in Freeport, Maine. Other good outlet centres are Kittery, Maine, and Manchester, New Hampshire.

'You want it, we got it': Boston's North End

### ELECTRIC GOODS

All mains-powered equipment is for 110 volts at 60 cycles, but battery-powered gadgets use international battery sizes and are often an excellent buy. As one of the major centres of America's high-tech industry, Boston has plenty of computer peripherals and software at bargain prices. Determine compatibility with overseas systems first.

### PHOTOGRAPHIC EQUIPMENT

The US is currently one of the cheapest places in the world to buy cameras and lenses, but always check on the lowest prices first. *Popular Photography*, a monthly magazine, carries dozens of ads for discounted equipment. These are usually in New York, but give an idea of a reasonable price range. Many shops will negotiate rather than lose a sale. Avoid shops in tourist areas, which may try to take advantage of foreigners.

Cameras sold in the US frequently have a designation different from the rest of the world. The Nikon 8008 is identical to the Nikon 801, but the shop assistants may not know this. Check on the specifications before you leave home. Remember, too, that the US designations are obvious to customs officials.

Film of all makes, types and formats is widely available at very low prices.

### SOUVENIRS

Maple syrup is perennially popular, and it is sold in quaint tin containers. Museum shops generally have very high-quality merchandise which is well-designed, functional and frequently educational. Crafts range from pottery to scrimshaw. Throughout northern New England, craft galleries are impossible to miss, and craft fairs are common.

New England is one of the few places in America with an abundance of antique shops. There are some very fine pieces to be found, but few bargains. Some of the best places for antiquing are in the Berkshires of western Massachusetts, Cape Cod (particularly along Route 6A and in Chatham), Connecticut's Litchfield County, and Newport, Rhode Island. Always ask for a written bill of sale guaranteeing authenticity.

For the sports fan, clothing in the colours of baseball and American football teams is available at most sports outfitters.

## BOSTON SHOPPING
### Boylston Street
Boylston runs parallel to Newbury Street just one block away. The Ritz-Carlton Hotel, probably Boston's finest, is just off one end of Boylston Street. Across the street next to the Ritz Parking Garage is **Firestone and Parson**, one of the city's best jewellery stores. Around the corner is **Shreve, Crump and Low**, a favourite old New England jewellery store which also sells antique silver and porcelain. A must is **FAO Schwartz** which has three floors of outrageous toys, including children's cars that are more expensive than some full-size production models! This store simply has to be seen to be believed. **Hermès** is a similarly extravagant adult version.

Boylston Street has many excellent stores

### Charles Street
From the corner of Boston Common and the Public Garden to Cambridge Street, Charles Street is a paradise for antique hunters. Dozens of small shops in basements, on second floors and down alleys offer an eclectic range of old things, from fine antiques to yesterday's ephemera.

### Copley Place
This glitzy shopping mall, together with The Shops on the Pru, at the corner of Copley Square, in Back Bay, houses 100 of the most elegant and expensive stores in Boston. The main tenant is **Nieman-Marcus**, with neighbours such as **Tiffany**, **Gucci**, **Louis Vuitton** and **Bally of Switzerland**. The centre also has a nine-screen cinema and several restaurants.

### Downtown Crossing
This is the heart of the central shopping district, anchored by two department stores, **Filene's** and **Macy's**, the biggest department store in New England.

Downtown Crossing is a pedestrian zone, and there are always lots of hawkers selling from pushcarts. Apart from the two main stores, there are several excellent small jewellery stores close by.

### Faneuil Hall Marketplace
Since opening in the 1960s, over a million people a month have visited this shopping area, which has become Boston's number-one tourist attraction. This is not the place to look for elegance or sophistication however. Most of the shops found here are popular chain stores such as the Body Shop and Express, although there are some worthwhile souvenirs to be found.

### Newbury Street

Without a doubt, this is the trendiest, classiest and most elegant shopping street in New England. Once making up an exclusive residential street in Back Bay, the brownstone houses are now home to **Brooks Brothers**, **Cartier**, **Burberry's** and a host of other fine stores, including **Louis**, which is the most chic men's store in town.

Newbury Street has more art galleries than any other stretch of road in America, but most of them are on upper floors, so remember to look up. Sidewalk cafés are interspersed with the elegant shops, giving the street a very European flavour. Newbury Street ends with a gigantic **Tower Records** store, where it is possible to satisfy the most esoteric musical tastes.

### Quincy Market

The Quincy Market building is full of food stalls, the Bull Market has pushcarts loaded with souvenirs and crafts, and the North and South Markets have a more traditional range of clothes shops. Here, too, you will find **The Sharper Image** (the ultimate in trendy adult toy stores) and **Banana Republic**, which was originally an army surplus store, but developed into a casual clothing store.

### CAMBRIDGE SHOPPING
### CambridgeSide

This is the region's newest shopping complex. The main tenants are **Filene's** (without the basement!) and **Sears**. Many of the smaller shops are more interesting, and include the up-scale clothiers **Abercrombie and Fitch**.

### Harvard Square

The most interesting shop here is the **Harvard Cooperative Society**,

Vibrant Quincy Market, a top tourist magnet

popularly known as the Coop – as in chicken! It was started back in 1882 as a non-profit store for students, and is now the biggest department store in the centre of Cambridge.

You can find just about anything here, especially the printed word – it has three floors of books. If you enjoy bookstores, Harvard Square is certainly the place to be. There are more bookstores per square foot here than in any other place in America. This is also the place where you can kit yourself out in a traditional 'preppie' outfit from one of the many clothing stores around the Square.

# Entertainment

*B*oston and Cambridge are, without doubt, the entertainment capitals of New England. Other cities have theatre, music and dance, but none can match the range or professionalism of Boston and Cambridge.

Both London's West End and Broadway shows are featured at theatres in Boston, complemented by a multitude of small theatres producing both experimental and traditional drama. The comedy clubs here are second only to New York and Los Angeles.

Music fans are well catered for, not only with an acoustically perfect Symphony Hall, but also with the outstanding Boston Symphony Orchestra, the renowned Boston Pops Orchestra, numerous jazz clubs, one of the great American folk clubs and a host of rock clubs. Although Boston has never been a particularly wild town at night, in recent years a number of establishments have emerged that make a dent, if not a hole, in this staid image.

For details of current offerings, the best source of information is either the Thursday 'Calendar' section of the *Boston Globe,* the weekly *Boston Phoenix,* published every Friday or *The Improper Bostonian*, published fortnightly. Boston by Phone is a 24-hour telephone information service. Dial (888) SEE-BOSTON and listen to the menu of options for access to detailed information. The website for Boston Convention and Visitors Bureau is at www.bostonusa.com. For up-to-the-minute details of current events the Boston Globe has a website at www.boston.com.

All year round, events take place throughout New England, from county fairs to film and jazz festivals. The dates and venues are different every year, but the various state offices of tourism will be able to provide information.

Tickets can usually be purchased at the venue or on the telephone by credit card, but it is increasingly common to buy tickets through a computerised ticket service. Most offer tickets by phone with a credit card. One of the biggest is **Ticketmaster** (tel: 617 931–2000). There is also **Ace Ticket Agency** (tel: 617 734–6666). Agencies usually add a service charge to the ticket price. Day-of-performance tickets are available at big discounts from **Bostix**, with ticket booths at Faneuil Hall Marketplace and Copley Square.

## MAJOR THEATRES
### Charles Playhouse
Home to *Sheer Madness*, the longest-running play in Boston.
*74–6 Warrenton Street. Tel: (617) 426–6912.*
### Colonial
*106 Boylston Street. Tel: (617) 426–9366.*
### Majestic Theater
*219 Tremont Street. Tel: (617) 824–8000.*
### Opera House
*539 Washington Street. Tel: (617) 426–5300.*
### Schubert Theater
*265 Tremont Street. Tel: (617) 426–4520.*
### Wang Center for the Performing Arts
*268 Tremont Street. Tel: (617) 482–9393.*
### Wilbur Theater
*246 Tremont Street. Tel: (617) 423–4008.*

## FRINGE THEATRES
### American Repertory Theater
*64 Brattle Street, Cambridge. Tel: (617) 495–2668.*
### Huntington Theater
*264 Huntington Avenue. Tel: (617) 266–0800.*

### The Lyric Stage
*140 Clarendon Street. Tel: (617) 437–7172.*
### Boston Center for the Arts
*539 Tremont Street. Tel: (617) 426–5000.*

Fourth of July festivities in Boston

The Boston Ballet Company performs at the Wang Center for the Performing Arts

## DINNER THEATRES
**Medieval Manor**
*246 East Berkeley Street.*
*Tel: (617) 423–4900.*
**Mystery Café**
*290 Congress Street.*
*Tel: (781) 320–0040.*
**Omni Parker House**
*Corner of Tremont and School Streets.*
*Tel: (617) 720–0108.*
**Rosie O'Grady's Blind Pig Saloon Dinner Theater**
*386 Market Street, Brighton.*
*Tel: (617) 723–3162.*
**The Terrace Room at the Boston Park Plaza**
*64 Arlington Street.*
*Tel: (617) 357–8384.*

## COMEDY CLUBS
**Catch a Rising Star**
*30 John F Kennedy Street, Cambridge.*
*Tel: (617) 661–9887.*

**Comedy Connection**
*245 Quincy Market Place.*
*Tel: (617) 248–9700.*
**Comedy Underground**
*246 Tremont Street.*
*Tel: (617) 426–3737.*
**Comedy Vault**
*124 Boylston Street,*
*Tel: (781) 729–2565.*
**Dick Doherty's Comedy Vault**
*124 Boylston Street.*
*Tel: (617) 267–6626.*
**The Improv Asylum**
*216 Hanover Street.*
*Tel: (617) 263–6887.*
**Nick's Comedy Stop**
*100 Warrenton Street.*
*Tel: (617) 482–0930.*

## CLASSICAL MUSIC
**Berklee College of Music**
*136 Massachusetts Avenue.*
*Tel: (617) 395–9228.*

**Boston Ballet**
Performs at the Wang Center.
*19 Clarendon Street.*
*Tel: (617) 695–6950.*
**Busch–Reisinger Museum**
*32 Quincy Street. Tel: (617) 495–9400.*
**Emmanuel Church**
*15 Newberry Street. Tel: (617) 536–3355.*
**Isabella Stewart Gardner Museum**
*280 The Fenway. Tel: (617) 566–1401.*
**Kings Chapel**
*Tremont/School streets. Tel: (617) 523–1749.*
**New England Conservatory of Music**
*30 Gainsborough Street. Tel: (617)*
*365–2412.*
**Opera Company of Boston**
*45 Franklin Street.*
*Tel: (617) 542–4912.*
**Symphony Hall**
*301 Massachusetts*
*Avenue. Tel: (617)*
*266–1492.*

**DANCING AND ROCK**
**Avalon**
*15 Landsdowne Street.*
*Tel: (617) 262–2424.*
**Axis**
*13 Landsdowne Street.*
*Tel: (617) 262–2424.*
**Copperfield's**
*98 Brookline Avenue.*
*Tel: (617)*
*247–8605.*
**Orpheum Theater**
*Hamilton Place off*
*Tremont Street.*
*Tel: (617)*
*482–0650.*
**Sugar Shack**
*1 Boylston Place.*
*Tel: (617)*
*351–2510.*

**Union**
*25 Boyleston Place. Tel: (617) 542–3689.*

**FOLK MUSIC**
**Passim**
*47 Palmer Street, Cambridge. Tel: (617)*
*492–7679.*

**JAZZ AND BLUES**
**Cosmopolitan**
*54 Canal Street. Tel: (617) 720–2889.*
**The Good Life**
*28 Kingston Street. Tel: (617) 451–2622.*
**Regattabar**
*Charles Hotel, 1 Bennett Street,*
*Cambridge. Tel: (617) 661–5050.*
**Ryles**
*212 Hampshire Street,*
*Cambridge. Tel: (617)*
*876–9330.*
**Wonder Bar**
*186 Harvard Avenue, Allston.*
*Tel: (617) 351–2665.*

# Festivals and Events

## JANUARY
**Massachusetts**
Chinese New Year, Boston (sometimes February).
**Vermont**
Annual Winter Carnival, Stowe.

## FEBRUARY
**Massachusetts**
Black History Month, Boston.
Winter Festival, Boston.
**New Hampshire**
Winter Carnival, Franklin.

## MARCH
**Massachusetts**
Boston Massacre Ceremony, Boston.
Fromm Concerts, Cambridge.
Great Chefs Fair, Boston.
New England Spring Garden and Flower Show, Boston.
St Patrick's Day, Boston.

## APRIL
**Maine**
Fisherman's Festival, Boothbay Harbor.
**Massachusetts**
Boston Marathon, Boston.
Daffodil Festival, Nantucket.
New England Folk Festival.
Patriot's Day, Lexington.
**Vermont**
Maple Sugar Festival, St Johnsbury.
State Maple Festival, St Albans.

## MAY
**Connecticut**
Lobster Festival, Mystic Seaport.
New England Fiddle Contest, Hartford.
**Maine**
Maine State Parade, Lewiston.
**Massachusetts**
Art Newberry Street, Boston.
Beacon Hill Hidden Garden Tour, Boston.
Berkshire Highland Games, Pittsfield.
Harvard Square May Fair, Cambridge.
Lilac Sunday at Arnold Arboretum, Boston.
Street Performers Festival, Boston.
**New Hampshire**
Sheep & Wool Festival, New Boston.

## JUNE
**Massachusetts**
Ancient and Honorable Artillery Company Parade, Boston.
Boston Globe Jazz Festival, Boston.
Bunker Hill Day, Boston.
Cambridge River Festival, Cambridge.
Dragon Boat Festival, Boston.
Victorian Promenade, Boston.
Harborlights Music Festival, Boston (June to September).
**New Hampshire**
Blessing of the Fleet, Portsmouth.
**Rhode Island**
Festival of Historic Homes, Providence.

## JULY
**Connecticut**
Ancient Fife & Drum Corps Parade and Muster, Deep River.
New England Arts and Crafts Festival, Milford.
**Massachusetts**
Bastille Day; Fourth of July; Harborfest; North End Festivals; Pops Esplanade Concerts, Boston.
Tanglewood Music Festival, Lenox.
**Rhode Island**
Black Ships Festival, Newport.
Newport Music Festival, Newport.

## AUGUST
### Connecticut
Quinnehtukqut Rendezvous & Native American Festival, Haddam.
### Maine
Fryeburg Fair, Fryeburg.
### Massachusetts
August Moon Festival, Boston.
Berkshire Crafts Fair, Great Barrington.
Caribbean Carnival Festival, Boston.
Faneuil Hall Marketplace Festival, Boston.
### New Hampshire
New Hampshire Craftsmen Fair, Sunapee.

## SEPTEMBER
### Massachusetts
Cranberry Festival, South Carver.
Gallops Island Cider Fest, Boston.
New England's Great State Fair, West Springfield.
### New Hampshire
World Mud Bowl Championships, North Conway.
### Rhode Island
Newport International Sailboat Show, Newport.
### Vermont
Dowsers Festival, Danville.

## OCTOBER
### Massachusetts
Columbus Day, Boston.
Harvest Weekend, Old Sturbridge Village.
Head of the Charles Regatta, Boston.
Worcester Music Festival, Worcester.
### New Hampshire
Fall Foliage Festival, Warner.
### Vermont
Northeast Kingdom Foliage Festival, Peacham, Groton.

## NOVEMBER
### Connecticut
Victorian Christmas, Gillette Castle, Hadlyme.
### Massachusetts
Boston Globe Book Festival, Boston.
International Auto Show, Boston.
Thanksgiving Day Celebration, Plymouth.
Veterans Day Parade, Boston.

## DECEMBER
### Massachusetts
New Year's Eve/First Night, Boston.
Tea Party Re-enactment, Boston.
### Rhode Island
Christmas in Newport, Newport.

### BEST FESTIVALS
Music lovers should not miss the Tanglewood Music Festival when the Boston Philharmonic Orchestra plays under the stars of the Berkshire Hills during the summer.

In Boston, the Boston Pops Orchestra starts its traditional concerts in the Shell on 4 July. Also in Boston, on 4 July, is Harborfest, a day-long festival throughout the city with several re-creations of New England's colonial past.

The Boston Marathon, one of the nation's most impressive athletic events, takes place on the third Monday of April. In late June Block Island, Rhode Island, is home to Race Week for hundreds of sail boats.

In late September, Vermont's Northeast Kingdom stages a week-long Fall Foliage Festival with country fairs in many of the region's delightful villages.

# Children

New England is the perfect place for youngsters to have fun and receive a painless education at the same time. The Greater Boston Visitors and Convention Bureau publishes *Kids Love Boston*, which is a children's guide to the area's major attractions.

In Massachusetts both Plimoth Plantation and Old Sturbridge Village present historically accurate information in the most entertaining way possible. Both of these living history sites should be on every parent's itinerary.

In Boston the **Children's Museum** (see page 31) is a perennial favourite with children of all ages. Next door, the **Computer Museum** (see page 35) is equally popular with young computer

Not for the timid: Boston's Museum of Science will provide plenty of memories

hacks – imagine playing a 3-D video game or flying a DC-10 into a volcano! The **Museum of Science** (see page 41) is also orientated towards the young, with plenty of hands-on exhibits on subjects as diverse as mathematics, optics, and the human body. Even the driest subject is fun. The world's largest Van der Graff generator, producing 15-foot bolts of lightening, pleases all ages, and younger children love to watch chicks hatch in the Giant Egg Incubator.

**Franklin Park Zoo**, which lies in part of the 'Emerald Necklace' (Boston's green belt), has a children's petting zoo, and in its African rainforest there are the sounds and sights of equatorial Africa, with 150 different animals from 50 species including gorillas. This is the largest artificial rainforest in the country. *Franklin Park, Blue Hill Avenue, Dorchester. Tel: (617) 442–2002. Open: Monday to Friday 10am–5pm, Saturday and Sunday 10am–6pm. Admission charge (free Tuesday afternoon).*

At the **New England Aquarium** (see page 42), there are dolphin and sea lion shows in Discovery, a floating theatre. Street performers are always fun to watch: in good weather stop by at **Faneuil Hall Marketplace**, Downtown Crossing or **Harvard Square** in Cambridge for great inexpensive entertainment. Before leaving Boston, a ride in the Public Garden's **swan boats** is an absolute must.

### Puppet Showplace Theater

Although some distance out of Boston in Brookline, the T station is right across the street, making it one of the most accessible attractions in the area. Every weekend fairy tales, ethnic folklore and Aesop's fables are presented in puppet shows. During the week there are displays of historic puppets and a small shop with toy puppets for sale. Just around the corner is **The Children's Book Shop** (tel: 617 734–7323), considered one of the best in the country. *The Puppet Showplace, 32 Station Street, Brookline. Tel: (617) 731–6400.*

### Ben and Jerry's Ice Cream Factory

in northern Vermont is every child's dream destination – the home of Ben and Jerry's ice cream ('best in the world', according to *Time* magazine). Factory tours include free samples. This is Vermont's number-two tourist attraction. *Route 100, Waterbury. Tel: (802) 244–1254. Open: daily 9am–6pm, to 9pm during July and August. Nominal admission charge.*

### Story Land

North of Conway in New Hampshire's White Mountains, Story Land is a fantasy park that brings fairy tales to life. Kids can travel by pumpkin coach to Cinderella's castle, take an African safari, ride on an antique train or even the Polar Coaster to the North Pole. There is also a petting farm with goats, sheep and pigs. *Story Land, Route 16, Glen. Tel: (603) 383–4293. Open: daily 9am–6pm from Father's Day to Labor Day; 10am–5pm weekends only, Labor Day to Columbus Day.*

### Clark's Trading Post

At the other end of the Kancamagus Highway is Clark's Trading Post in North Woodstock. This small theme park offers rides on the White Mountain Central Railroad; a standard-gauge

Hands-on displays at the Computer Museum

wood-burning steam engine pulls the train over a covered bridge by the Pemigewasset River.

Back at the trading post there is a family of native New Hampshire black bears, which perform throughout the day, a Mystical Mansion, a Rustic House that never fails to delight children with its bizarre surprises, and the Mill Pond Bumper Boats, which help visitors to cool off on a hot day. *Clark's Trading Post, Route 3, North Woodstock. Tel: (603) 745–8913. Open: July and August, daily 9am–5.45pm; weekends only from Memorial Day to the end of June and Labor Day to mid-October.*

# Sport

New Englanders are an understated bunch – except when it comes to sports. Loud and loyal fans of their sports teams, and active participants in a variety of outdoor activities, they love their sports. And there are a number of sports to love. New England has some of the nation's most admired professional sports teams and a long tradition of college sports excellence. The huge quilt of forests, rivers, mountains and lakes that form the New England landscape also boasts a bounty of recreational activities, which provide wonderful diversions for intrepid travellers.

## SPECTATOR SPORTS

### The Boston Marathon

Held every year since 1897, this is the world's oldest annual event and part of the Boston way of life. Every Patriot's Day both spectators and participants gather for this impressive event.

### Baseball

Few teams have a more illustrious history than the Boston Red Sox, New England's only major league baseball team. The Red Sox won the first World Series ever played – in 1903 – and have had some of baseball's greatest play for them, including Babe Ruth, Ted Williams and Wade Boggs.

The baseball season begins early in April and ends the first weekend in October. Teams from both the American League and National League bat it out on Astroturf and natural grass, playing about 80 home games a year. In Boston, the Red Sox play at the fabulous Fenway Park, on 'old-fashioned' grass, in the heart of Kenmore Square (tel: 617 267–8661 or 617 267–1700 for tickets).

New England is also home to a number of minor league teams in small towns throughout the region; these provide the training grounds for the next generation of major league stars. Check local listings for minor league games in cities from Burlington to Pawtucket.

### Basketball

America's most famous professional basketball team, the Boston Celtics, are tied to the heart and soul of Boston. Named for the Bay City's substantial Irish population, the Celtics have won 16 National Basketball Association championships, more than any other professional team. The regular NBA season runs from October until April, with championship playoffs continuing until June. The Celtics play at the FleetCenter (tel: 617 624–6050).

### American football

After years of dwelling at the bottom of the ranks, the New England Patriots are struggling towards success in pro football. The team has made it to the Super Bowl once in its history, in 1986, only to lose to the Chicago Bears.

Twenty-eight National Football League teams take to the field (called the gridiron) every year. Pre-season action begins in early August. The regular season runs from early September to late December. Playoffs and the Super Bowl take the season into late January. The Patriots play at Sullivan Stadium in Foxboro, about 45

Spend a balmy summer's evening watching a Red Sox game at Fenway Park baseball stadium

minutes south of Boston (tel: 508 543–8220).

The Patriots aren't the only game in town, however. Every autumn, loyal alumni from New England's many colleges head for university stadiums throughout the region. Here, tradition plays as much a role as the game itself, as old friendships – and rivalries – are rekindled. Perhaps the most famous of these is the annual Harvard/Yale game, known simply as The Game. The competition, more than 100 years old, is the nation's longest-standing intercollegiate sporting event, pitting athletes from two of America's Ivy League universities against each other in a battle more over prestige and honour than athletic prowess. For ticket information, call Harvard on (617) 495–2211 or Yale on (203) 432–1400. Check local listings for other college games.

### Ice hockey

Ice hockey, known simply as hockey in the US, migrated south from Canada a century ago and settled happily in the cold New England winter landscape. Today, it is among the most popular games in the region.

Two professional teams and scores of collegiate teams constitute the core of spectator opportunities. From November to April, the National Hockey League draws thousands to arenas to witness ice hockey being played at its best. The Boston Bruins, a founding team of the National Hockey League, play in the FleetCenter (tel: 617 624–1000). The Hartford Wolfpack (tel: 820 246–7825) take to the ice at the Hartford Civic Center in Hartford, Connecticut.

Some of America's finest collegiate hockey is also played on arenas throughout New England.

Fishing in idyllic surroundings on the Mohawk Trail in Massachusetts

## OTHER SPORTS

A number of other spectator sports rank among New Englanders' favourites, from horse racing to *jai alai* (pronounced high-a-lie) – an unusual court game resembling handball, in which players with long curved wicker baskets catch and throw a hard ball against a wall. Local chambers of commerce or visitors bureaus can give you the specifics.

It's not difficult to see why so many New Englanders enjoy the outdoors. The region is full of summer and winter activities, from sailing along the Cape Cod coast to skiing down Stowe

Mountain's well-groomed slopes. Following is a sampling of summer and winter sports.

### Swimming
On a hot summer day, nothing could be finer than lounging along a Cape Cod beach, plunging into the icy waters off the Maine coast, or taking a dip in Vermont's Lake Champlain. Most of New England's best beaches are open to the public, so pack a picnic, bring plenty of tanning lotion – and get there early before the crowds. Note that, to locals, a 'beach' could refer to an area of imported sand on the edge of a lake where everyone swims.

### Sailing
If you arrived by yacht, or you just love to sail, New England's wrinkled coast-line provides an ocean of opportunity for enjoying the open waters. Charters are available, and most harbours have a marina or dock to pull into for the night. For sailing without the salt, take advantage of the region's bounty of inland waters.

### Other water sports
Surfers ride the waves off the coasts of Maine, Nantucket and Martha's Vineyard, while a growing legion of windsurfers can be found just about anywhere there is water. New England also enjoys excellent fishing, whether in freshwater streams and lakes or surf-casting and deep-sea fishing. Wherever there is a harbour, someone will likely be offering fishing charters. Consult the local tourist bureau for specifics.

### Golf and tennis
Like most American regions, New England is packed with championship

golf courses and excellent tennis facilities. The Professional Golf Association hosts tournaments at Pleasant Valley near Worcester, Massachusetts, and at a designated course in Hartford, Connecticut. The Country Club at Brookline near Boston recently hosted the US Open golf championships. The Yellow Pages has listings of both public and private golf courses.

For racquet enthusiasts, the region has a rich history of tennis excellence, dating back to the inception of the US Pro Championships. The annual event, held at the Longwood Cricket Club near Boston, is one of professional tennis's longest-standing tournaments. The Tennis Hall of Fame in Newport, Rhode Island, hosts America's only grass-court tournament, just after Wimbledon. Visitors can find courts at many of New England's resorts and hotels; most city parks also have several courts available. For more information contact the New England Tennis Association (tel: 617 964–2030).

### Skiing

Whether you're a downhill or a cross-country skier, New England can accommodate you. From November to April, you can ski in every one of the region's states at resorts that offer the finest skiing in the East.

For Alpiners, the best skiing is up north. Stowe, Killington and Stratton Mountain are among the best ski resorts in Vermont, while New Hampshire boasts Waterville Valley and Maine claims Sugarloaf and Sunday River. There are dozens of other venues as well.

Nordic skiers can enjoy a day in the woods at a number of ski-touring centres throughout the region, including

Golf at Oak Bluffs, Martha's Vineyard

The Hermitage near Dover, Vermont. For the more daring, there are trips into the back country in one of the region's mountain parks and preserves (never go without a guide).

If you are thinking of a back-country trip, contact the Appalachian Club (tel: 603 466–2727). It maintains several huts that stay open in winter for skiers and snowshoers. For all ability levels, Pathways Through Vermont operates in both winter and summer (tel: 802 824–3830).

For details of cycling, hiking, canoeing and kayaking see **Getting Away From it All**, page 148.

---

**SKI INFO**

Vermont Ski Areas Association, 26 State Street, Montpelier, Vermont 05602. Tel: (800) 223–2439 (toll free). Appalachian Mountain Club, Box 298, Pinkham Notch, NH 03581. Tel: (603) 466–2727, or AMC, 5 Joy Street, Boston, Massachusetts 02108.
Massachusetts Ski Hotline, tel: (800) 227–MASS.

# Food and Drink

New England has a reputation for good, honest, traditional food. Seafood is particularly good, with dishes like New England clam chowder (a thick milk-based soup), fish cakes and fresh boiled lobster. Other regional specialities are Boston baked beans, Indian pudding and Boston cream pie. 'Raw bars' serve fresh raw shellfish such as oysters. Clambakes are a New England tradition that should not be missed if the opportunity arises.

Not all New England restaurants are good, of course. Vast numbers of eating establishments rely more on quantity than quality and serve greasy, unimaginative food. Some American eating habits may seem curious to visitors. Biscuits are like unsweetened scones, and they are usually served smothered in thick white gravy – very often for breakfast! Fruit is considered an appropriate accompaniment to any meal, so don't be too surprised if your bacon and eggs come with a fruit salad on the same plate.

Snackers's stop-off

## FAST FOOD

McDonald's, KFC (Kentucky Fried Chicken) and Pizza Hut dominate the world market, and they are equally dominant in New England. Fortunately, changing tastes and attitudes have forced the greasy hamburgers with fries to compete with chicken breast sandwiches and salads. McDonald's has even introduced a low-fat hamburger, the McLean Burger. Wendy's, Hardee's, Burger King and Jack in the Box provide variations of the same products at more or less the same price.

## COFFEE SHOPS

The coffee shop chains are one step above the fast-food operations and include Friendly's, Howard Johnson's (Ho Jo's) and Denny's. They are often open 24 hours a day and serve perfectly edible, if unmemorable, food. They all have inexpensive children's menus, and you need never feel embarrassed at having boisterous children at your table.

## DINERS

The diner is a very American institution. Diners are not a lot different from coffee shops, generally smaller with a long counter to sit at. The traditional diner was designed to look like a railroad dining car with lots of chrome and a juke box. They always served good, basic, cheap food without any frills. There are still a few around, but be careful. Diners have been 'yuppiefied', and they will not necessarily be the good, cheap eats you expect.

## BREAKFAST

Diners and coffee shops (not the chains) are the best places for breakfast, and it is often served 24 hours a day. Eggs are the mainstay, and you can have them as omelettes, scrambled, boiled, poached or fried any number of ways: *sunny-side up* (cooked on one side only), *over easy* (flipped over so that the white is fully cooked but the yolk is still runny), *over medium* (one step beyond the above), *over hard* (both white and yolk are solid). The eggs are invariably served with hash-brown potatoes, a choice of sausage, ham or bacon, and white or wholewheat bread or an English muffin.

At weekends breakfast is eclipsed by brunch at the better restaurants. Usually served between 10am and 3pm, this leisurely meal is an elaborate, substantial breakfast/lunch, accompanied by champagne.

Fit for a feast: Atlantic lobster

Coffee is the main beverage and it varies dramatically in quality from brown water to something a spoon will stand up in. As a rule of thumb, the cheaper the restaurant, the weaker the coffee. This may have something to do with the American tradition of the 'bottomless cup' – refills are free for as long as you sit. Tea is less popular, and it is easy to see why. A cup of tea consists of a tea bag in tepid water. Water will continue to be provided until no more colour can be drained from the bag.

Every part of the meal involves decisions. There is no such thing as a simple cup of tea. Do you want Darjeeling, English breakfast, Earl Grey, camomile, Constant Comment, ginseng? You want milk in it? How about half-and-half, 1 per cent, non-fat, regular, vitamin D, non-dairy creamer? Ordering the simplest meal can be complicated.

## LOCAL FOOD
Fresh produce is always close at hand, and the Atlantic provides some of the finest fish and shellfish available. Over 23 million pounds of lobster are caught in Maine every year, in addition to excellent clams, mussels and scallops. The fish includes cod, for which Massachusetts is famous, haddock, sole, flounder and bass.

Agriculture is not big in New England, as it has neither the soil nor the climate to be a major producer. However, the coastal bogs of Massachusetts provide the world's biggest supply of cranberries, without which every American's Thanksgiving dinner would be incomplete. These tart red berries are used for their juice and to make a sauce or jelly to accompany roast turkey. New England apples are exceptionally good, and there is a big cider industry (American cider is really apple juice, but hard cider and applejack are alcoholic).

Wherever you decide to eat in New England, you will almost certainly eat well – and for much less than you would pay for the equivalent meal at home.

# Restaurants

The symbols below indicate restaurant price. The $ sign represents the cost of a 3-course meal without wine.

$ under $15
$$ under $25
$$$ under $50
$$$$ over $50

## BOSTON AREA

**Aujourd'hui $$$$**
A spectacular view over the Public Garden combined with above-average nouvelle cuisine.
*Four Seasons Hotel, 200 Boylston Street. Tel: (617) 351–2071.*

**Bangkok Cuisine $$**
Great Thai food, near Symphony Hall.
*177A Massachusetts Avenue. Tel: (617) 262–5377.*

**Bertucci's Brick Oven Pizzeria $**
Popular, above-average pizza place.
*Locations throughout Boston.*

**Biba $$$$**
Eclectic cuisine in stylish surroundings.
*272 Boylston Street. Tel: (617) 426–7878.*

**Boco Grande $**
Good, fresh self-service Mexican food.
*149 First Street, Cambridge. Tel: (617) 354–5550.*

**Caffe Vittoria $**
Inexpensive Italian food in Little Italy with lots of atmosphere.
*296 Hanover Street. Tel: (617) 227–7606.*

**Charlie's Sandwich Shoppe $**
Basic coffee shop food, also serves good breakfasts.
*429 Columbus Avenue. Tel: (617) 536–7669.*

**Chau Chow $**
Cantonese food at its best in less than salubrious surroundings.
*52 Beach Street. Tel: (617) 426–6266.*

**Chez Nous $$$$**
Excellent nouvelle cuisine in intimate atmosphere.
*147 Huron Avenue, Cambridge. Tel: (617) 864–6670.*

**Copley's $$$**
Traditional New England cuisine in Old Boston atmosphere.
*Copley Plaza Hotel, 138 St James Avenue. Tel: (617) 267–5300.*

**Daily Catch $$**
Great squid and fresh fish.
*Several locations throughout Boston.*

**Dali $$**
A good Spanish restaurant.
*415 Washington Street, Somerville. Tel: (617) 661–3254.*

**Davide $$$**
Excellent Northern Italian cuisine.
*326 Commercial Avenue. Tel: (617) 227–5745.*

**The Elephant Walk $$**
Aristocratic Cambodian cuisine with traditional and original French.
*900 Beacon Street. Tel: (617) 247–1500.*

**Giacomo's $$**
Great seafood.
*355 Hanover Street. Tel: (617) 523–9026.*

**Hammersley's Bistro $$$–$$$$**
One of the great Boston restaurants serving French-influenced dishes.
*533 Tremont Street. Tel: (617) 423–2700.*

**India Castle $$**
*928 Massachusetts Avenue, Cambridge. Tel: (617) 864–8100.*

**Jasper's $$$$**
Classic New England food in elegant surroundings.
*240 Commercial Street. Tel: (617) 523–1126.*

**Legal Seafoods $$$**
Universally claimed to serve the best

seafood in town. All the locations are always crowded.
*Locations throughout Boston.*

**Locke-Ober Café $$$$**
A classic Boston restaurant formal to the point of being stuffy, serving American food in the New England tradition.
*3 Winter Place. Tel: (617) 542–1340.*

**Maison Robert $$$$**
Classic French cuisine in very elegant surroundings. A less formal, and less expensive dining room can be found downstairs.
*45 School Street. Tel: (617) 227–3370.*

**Massimino's $$**
Good inexpensive Italian food.
*207 Endicott Street. Tel: (617) 523–5959.*

**Milk Street Café $**
Financial District cafeteria open for breakfast and lunch, serving excellent inexpensive food including kosher meals.
*50 Milk Street. Tel: (617) 542–3663.*

**Parker's $$$**
Great for brunch.
*Omni Parker House, 60 School Street. Tel: (617) 227–8600.*

**Pho Pasteur $**
Theatre District Vietnamese restaurant.
*8 Kneeland Street. Tel: (617) 451–0247.*

**Ritz Café $$$**
Always good food in very elegant surroundings.
*Ritz Carlton Hotel, 15 Arlington Street. Tel: (617) 536–5700.*

**Ritz Dining Room $$$$**
Outstanding service, surroundings and food make this one of Boston's most memorable dining experiences.
*Ritz Carlton Hotel, 15 Arlington Street. Tel: (617) 536–5700.*

**Season's $$$$**
A training ground for the great Boston chefs, and it remains one of the city's great restaurants.

*Bostonian Hotel, 9 Blackstone Street. Tel: (617) 523–3600.*

**Sultan's Kitchen $**
Downtown lunch spot serving good Turkish food.
*72 Broad Street. Tel: (617) 338–7819.*

**Union Oyster House $$**
A landmark Boston restaurant.
*41 Union Street. Tel: (617) 227–2750.*

**Upstairs at the Pudding $$$$**
A Harvard University tradition.
*10 Holyoke Street, Cambridge. Tel: (617) 864–1933.*

## OUTSIDE BOSTON
**Al Forno $$$**
Superb Northern Italian food but no reservations can mean long waits.
*577 South Main Street, Providence. Tel: (401) 273–9760.*

**Arrows $$$$**
New American cuisine.
*Berwick Street, Ogunquit, Maine. Tel: (207) 361–1100.*

**Chanticleer $$$$**
Classic French cuisine.
*9 New Street, Nantucket. Tel: (508) 257–6231.*

**Chillingsworth $$$$**
Nouvelle French cuisine.
*2449 Main Street, Brewster. Tel: (508) 896–3460.*

**Topper's $$$$**
Exceptional French cuisine.
*120 Wauwinet Road, Nantucket. Tel: (508) 228–8768*

**21 Federal $$$$**
New American cuisine.
*21 Federal Street, Nantucket. Tel: (508) 228–2121.*

**White Horse Tavern $$$$**
Traditional New England food and atmosphere.
*26 Marlborough Street, Newport. Tel: (401) 849–3600.*

# MAPLE SYRUP

As the sap rises every spring, while snow is still on the ground, hundreds of sugarhouses throughout northern New England fire up their boilers to produce the sweet amber syrup of the sugar maple (as well as sugar and sweets/candy).

Vermont alone accounts for over half a million gallons a year, more than any other state in the nation. Each mature tree produces about 10 gallons of sap, and it takes 30 to 40 gallons to produce one gallon of syrup. The rest is lost to evaporation. Traditionally the sap was collected in individual buckets attached to each tree, but now plastic tubing connects several trees to a collecting tank or even directly to the sugarhouse.

For the 'sugaring-off' process, the sap is boiled in large, flat evaporating pans over wood or gas fires for up to 24 hours until it thickens. The syrup is filtered and graded according to colour. The choicest maple syrup is the lightest in colour.

Most sugarhouses welcome visitors. Look out for 'Maple Sugar' signs on the country roads, or ask at the local general store. Better yet, find them listed in *Maple Sugarhouses*, published by the Vermont Department of Agriculture, 116 State Street, Montpelier, VT 05602 (tel: 802 828–2416). Listings are by town and give information on the size of the sugarhouses, methods of operation and times of tours.

The season traditionally begins on the first Tuesday in March, but in reality it needs freezing nights and a daytime temperature of 40–50°F to make the sap run. In southern Vermont this is usually at the end of February, through to late March or early April in the north. The season usually lasts from three to four weeks.

You can still experience the process out of season at one of the museums devoted to the subject. The New England Maple Museum, Route 7, Pittsford, Vermont (tel: 802 483–9414) is full of old artefacts and even includes a free syrup tasting. The Maple Grove Maple Museum is the northern equivalent off highway I–91 in St Johnsbury.

Far left: maple syrup exhibit at the popular Fryeburg Fair, Maine, held in early October.
Above: local produce and syrup in Lyme, New Hampshire.
Left: maple syrup comes in all shapes and sizes

# Hotels and Accommodation

New England has an enormous variety of accommodation, and most of it is relatively inexpensive compared to the rest of the world. It is also of an almost universally high standard. Even the cheapest places are clean and well-appointed. (This is not the case with inner-city residential hotels, which cater to transients and often look as though they went out of business decades ago.)

## MOTELS

The motel, of course, is the American lodging *par excellence*. For the budget-conscious traveller, these are by far the best places to stay. The chain motels are perhaps the most predictable for quality, but there are fewer in New England than in other areas of America so it pays to book ahead. They all provide a clean, simply decorated room, usually with the choice of twin or double beds. There is always a television, a telephone in all but the most basic, and always a bathroom or shower and toilet adjoining the room.

The difference between the cheapest and the next category up is very slight. There may be a swimming pool and you may get a sachet of shampoo in the bathroom, but these refinements can cost $20–$30 more without any increase in basic comfort.

Payment is usually in advance, and rooms will be held only until 5pm unless the reservation is secured with a credit card.

Motels tend to be on the outskirts of town on the main roads, and are rarely convenient for sightseeing. If you have a car, this should not present a problem. Motels are usually very well advertised with huge roadside signs. Most towns have a motel strip (Boston is a notable exception). The closest motel area to Boston is north on Route 1, well outside the city limits. If in doubt, any local should be able to tell you where to go. Breakfast is never included at motels, but there is usually a restaurant close by and there will be vending machines for soft drinks. Complimentary coffee is

Well-disguised rural inn

sometimes provided in the lobby (reception).

Most motels in New England are privately owned, but there are a few chains. Good, very inexpensive chains are:
**Motel 6** (tel: 800 437–7486)
**Days Inn** (tel: 800 325–2525)
**Super 8** (tel: 800 800–8000).
Also very good but not as cheap are:
**Travelodge** (tel: 800 255–3050)
**Comfort Inn** (tel: 800 221–2222)
**Best Western** (tel: 800 528–1234)
**Howard Johnson's** (tel: 800 654–2000).

## BED AND BREAKFAST INNS
Most villages have an inn, usually by the village green, which will often date back to colonial times. If modern comforts are not a primary concern, then these antique-filled historic buildings will provide surroundings steeped in atmosphere. The food served is usually good, hearty home cooking, and meal times provide a perfect opportunity to experience Yankee hospitality.

There are so many bed and breakfast inns in New England that the best way to get accurate current information is to contact the relevant state tourist office.

## HOTELS
Full-service hotels are much more expensive than motels, and they are generally only found in the major cities. There are some excellent hotels in New England for those who can afford them, although few could be described as classic. Nevertheless, for the ultimate in both luxury and service, these are the places to stay:
**Boston** The Bostonian,
   Copley Plaza,
   The Ritz-Carlton;

The elegant Ritz-Carlton Dining Room requires appropriate dress

**Cambridge** The Charles Hotel;
**Cape Cod** Chatham Bars Inn;
**Deerfield** The Deerfield Inn;
**Martha's Vineyard** Charlotte Inn;
**Hanover, NH** The Hanover Inn;
**Hartford, CT** The J P Morgan Hotel;
**Manchester, VT** The Equinox;
**Newport, RI** The Inn at Castle Hill,
    The Viking.

Even in hotels of this quality, breakfast is rarely included in the price, although there is a growing trend to include a continental breakfast at some hotels.

The Boston Harbor Hotel at Rowes Wharf

## RESORT HOTELS

Also at the top end of the market are resort hotels, which not only provide deluxe service and surroundings but also a range of sports, including tennis and golf, and often spa facilities. Once you've checked into one of these luxury resorts, there is no need to set foot in the outside world again until your money runs out. Some of the best resort hotels are:

The Balsams in the White Mountains, New Hampshire;

The Canyon Ranch in the Berkshires, New Hampshire;

Mountain Green Ski and Golf Resort, Killington, Vermont;

Mount Washington Hotel and Resort, Bretton Woods, New Hampshire;

The Norwich Inn, Norwich, Connecticut.

Most of the big international hotel chains have properties in Boston and New England, and these provide a more reasonably priced alternative to the resorts without the glamour of a landmark building. They are usually well-located near main tourist attractions:

**Doubletree** (tel: 800 528–0444)

**Hilton** (tel: 800 445–8667)

**Holiday Inn** (tel: 800 465–4329)

**Hyatt** (tel: 800 228–900)
**Marriot** (tel: 800 228–9290)
**Ramada** (tel: 800 272–6232)
**Sheraton** (tel: 800 325–3535).

## RESERVATIONS

It is always wise to make reservations, particularly during the peak season and special events. In making reservations for any accommodation make sure it is in a convenient location. Ask plenty of questions. It is also worth asking if there are any special rates available. Many places will give significant discounts rather than lose the business; it never does any harm to ask.

Several chains offer discounts if vouchers are purchased outside of the US. These include:
**Howard Johnson's** – Freedom North America;
**Vagabond** – Discover America Hotel Pass;
**Tourcheck America** – handles bookings for Best Western, Hilton, Holiday Inn, Ramada, Travelodge and Quality Inn hotels and motels.

Most travel agents should be aware of these programmes and have vouchers available for purchase.

Travellers who purchase their travel tickets from a Thomas Cook network location are entitled to use the services of any other Thomas Cook network location, free of charge, to make hotel reservations (see the **Practical Guide**, page 186).

Long-distance calls from in-room telephones can be outrageously expensive, and there is often a charge even for reverse-charge or credit-card calls. Always find out what these charges are to avoid a nasty shock when it's too late. All hotels and motels have public telephones available in the lobby areas.

Many hotels do not charge for local calls, but paradoxically it is usually the cheaper places that have this policy. Again, check before use.

In-room mini-bars are another big profit-maker for hotels. Drinks are so cheap in most New England states that if you enjoy a nightcap it is almost cheaper to buy a full bottle at a supermarket than to buy a miniature from a mini-bar.

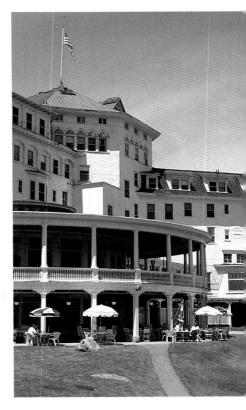

The grand turn-of-the-century Mount Washington Hotel, with landscaped grounds

# On Business

*B*usiness practices in the United States are the same as in Europe. International business in the English-speaking world has become so uniform it can be difficult to know which country you are in.

The general visa and immigration rules (see Practical Guide) apply to business travellers intending to leave the country within a 6-month period. Special visas are necessary for extended stays and for permission to work in the United States. The availability of these is dependent upon circumstances, and advice should be sought from the closest American Consulate.

Boston is the only major international business centre in New England. The main industries are computers, publishing, education and fishing. Two hundred million pounds of fish are landed annually, and inevitably there are extensive fish-freezing and cold-storage plants. Other important industries include: printing, shipbuilding, sugar-refining, boot and shoe manufacture, electrical machinery, textiles, bakery products, confectionery, cutlery, leather, plastics, chemicals, furniture, foundry and machine-shop products, woollens, worsteds and meat packing.

Hartford, Connecticut, is the world centre for the insurance industry. It is also the home of United Technologies. Other significant industries include manufacturing, finance, precision tools, brushes, revolvers, dishwashers, glass-making machines, power transmission chains, airplane engines and propellers, counting devices, nails, castings, electrical equipment and auto parts. Hartford is also the centre of the tobacco-growing region.

## BANKS

Major European banks are represented in Boston, and there are numerous New England banks for local currency transactions. Few banks have foreign exchange facilities, but any bank can receive payments wired from overseas. It is preferable to have the money wired in US dollars to avoid unnecessary delays and often high bank charges. Banking hours are generally from 9am to 4pm, but this varies from bank to bank. The tendency is for banks to stay open longer.

## BUSINESS HOURS

Most offices are open Monday to Friday from 9am to 5pm. However, it is not at all unusual to find people working beyond these times and over weekends. Most business support services, including office supply shops, close over the weekend. Post offices are open briefly on Saturday mornings in most towns.

## BUSINESS MEDIA
### Boston (newspapers/magazines)
*Adweek/New England, Banker and Tradesman, Boston Business Journal, Boston Globe, Boston Herald, Harvard Business Review, Industry, New England Business, New England Economic Review.*
### (TV/radio)
CNN – cable television channel giving regular business and stock market news throughout the day.
WBZ-AM 1030 – ABC affiliate radio

programme with occasional business coverage.

WHDH-AM 850 – NBC affiliate as above.

WUMB-FM 91.9 – public broadcasting station carries BBC World Service News.

## Hartford
*The Business Journal, Business Times, The Hartford Courant.*

## CONFERENCE/EXHIBITION SITES
### Boston
**Bayside Expo Center**, *200 Mount Vernon Street. Tel: (617) 477–6554, fax: (617) 265–8434.*

**Boston Park Plaza Hotel and Towers**, *64 Arlington Street. Tel: (617) 426–2000, fax: (617) 654–1999.*

**Hynes Convention Center**, *900 Boylston Street. Tel: (617) 954–2000, fax: (617) 954–2125.*

**Marriot Hotel – Copley Place**, *110 Huntington Avenue. Tel: (617) 236–5800, fax: (617) 236–5885.*

**Northeast Trade Center and Exhibition Hall**, *100 Sylvan Road, Woburn. Tel: (617) 935–8090.*

**World Trade Center**, *164 Northern Avenue. Tel: (617) 439–5000, fax: (617) 439–5090.*

**Westford Regency Inn and Conference Center**, *219 Littleton Road, Westford, MA 01886. Tel: (508) 692–8200.*

### Hartford
**Hartford Civic Center**, *1 Civic Center Plaza. Tel: (860) 249–6333, fax: (860) 241–4226.*

### Providence, Rhode Island
**Providence Civic Center**, 1 LaSalle Square. *Tel: (401) 331–0700.*

## INTERNATIONAL COURIER SERVICES
**DHL Worldwide Express**, *tel: (1–800) 225–5345*; **Federal Express**, *tel: (1–800) 238–5355*; **United States Postal Service**, *tel: (1–800) 222–1811.*

## SECRETARIAL SERVICES
Most major city-centre hotels have at least basic executive services. Virtually all hotels now have fax machines for guests, many have copy facilities, several have full secretarial services available and a growing number have in-room modems. There is an abundance of secretarial help available listed in the Yellow Pages. The HQ Headquarters Companies, 124 Mt Auburn Street, Cambridge (tel: 617 547–0222), offer a full range of services.

## TRANSLATION SERVICES
**AT & T Language Line Services** *(tel: 1–800 752–6096, ext 409 – toll free)*; **Harvard Translations** *(tel: 617 868–6800).*

## TRANSPORTATION
Aircraft charter companies providing helicopters, Lear jets and smaller fixed-wing aircraft:
### Boston
**Business Helicopters** *(tel: 617 274–1230).*

**Executive Fliteways** *(tel: 1–800 533–3363).*

**Flight Time International** *(tel: 781 891–0405).*

**Wiggins Airways** *(tel: 800 877–5690).*

**Delta Helicopter** *(tel : 617 776–6670).*

### Hartford
**Executive Airlines** (tel: 800 393–2884).

**Million Air** *(tel: 203 548–9334).*

# Practical Guide

## CONTENTS

## ARRIVING

### Entry requirements

Travellers from Australia and South Africa will need a visa. Travellers from the UK, New Zealand and Canada do not require a visa for stays up to 90 days, but will be asked to complete a visa waiver form by their airline or shipping company. All travellers must be in possession of a passport (valid for at least 6 months except in the case of UK passport holders) and a ticket for return or onward travel from the USA.

Travellers who require visas should obtain them in their country of residence, as they are difficult to obtain elsewhere. In the UK your Thomas Cook travel consultant can advise.

While in the USA, visitors can take a side trip overland or by sea into Canada or Mexico and re-enter without a visa, within their overall 90-day stay.

Immigration laws are both complicated and strictly enforced, and it is advisable to check with the American Consulate well before departure.

### By air

Logan International is the main airport for international flights into New England, handling over 60 airlines. Virtually all international visitors will come through Logan.

Bradley International Airport in Connecticut and Bangor International Airport in Maine handle some international traffic, but they are mainly used for domestic routings. Sometimes it can be less expensive to fly into New York's Kennedy Airport and get a connecting flight to one of the New England airports.

Domestic flights are generally very expensive, with the exception of the services between Boston and New York.

Boston's T service is efficient, clean and user-friendly; its four lines intersect downtown

If planning short hops within New England or flying in from another state, it is advisable to purchase a ticket before arrival. Airport taxes are included in the price of the ticket. Several airlines offer Visit USA passes, and travel agents should be able to advise on the best deals.

Logan International Airport has five terminals. Terminals B, C and E serve international scheduled flights. A free bus service links them, with a separate free service for disabled travellers. Terminals C and E have foreign exchange facilities and information booths, although neither are 24-hour.

There are duty-free shops in Departures. All terminals cater for disabled travellers, with lifts, ramps, adapted toilets and amplified phones. Terminal C has a 24-hour nursery, and all terminals have catering facilities.

The airport stands on a peninsula facing the city. It therefore takes only 7 minutes to reach the city centre by the water shuttle (take the free bus from terminal to shuttle departure point), but 30 minutes by taxi and 20 to 30 minutes by the MBTA, called the T (Blue line –

free bus from terminals to T station). The T is by far the cheapest option. There are many express bus services from the airport to outlying areas of Boston (for information call from the airport on freephone 1–800–23–LOGAN).

Any Thomas Cook Network travel location will offer airline ticket re-routing and revalidation free of charge to MasterCard cardholders and to travellers who have purchased their travel tickets through Thomas Cook. Ask your Thomas Cook travel consultant for details of the local network licensee when making your travel bookings.

**By rail**

Amtrak rail services connect Boston South and Boston Back Bay stations with Providence, New Haven and New York City, and New Haven and other New England towns with Montreal. Amtrak timetables are published in the *Thomas Cook Overseas Timetable* (see page 188).

**CAMPING**

New England in the summer is ideal for camping holidays, and outside the major

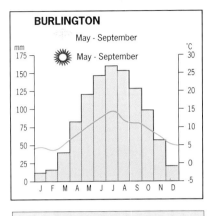

BURLINGTON
May - September
May - September

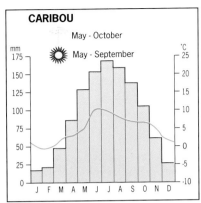

CARIBOU
May - October
May - September

**WEATHER CONVERSION CHART**
25.4mm = 1 inch
°F = 1.8 × °C + 32

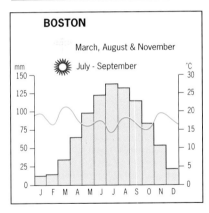

BOSTON
March, August & November
July - September

cities there is no shortage of campsites.

State parks and national forests have excellent camping facilities, but reservations must be made if you are planning a visit during the peak season. Information can be obtained from the state tourism offices. Camper vans – called motor homes or RVs (recreational vehicles) in the US – are available for hire from specialist companies. One of the largest is **Cruise America** (tel: 800 327–7778). Smaller local companies are listed in the Yellow Pages under Motor Homes – Renting and Leasing. It may be cheaper to pre-book through your own travel agent; for instance Thomas Cook in the UK offers this and other options in its *America for the Independent Traveller* brochure.

**CHILDREN**
Many hotels provide cribs for free, and extra beds for older children sharing their parents' room at a nominal charge. Larger hotels offer safe and reliable babysitting services. Many restaurants have children's menus. Highchairs are universally available. Children are not allowed in bars unless meals are served.

Diapers (nappies) and food for infants are available at any supermarket or drugstore, and in most towns can be found 24 hours a day in at least one convenience store. Baby milk, called infant formula, is available in several dairy and non-dairy varieties. Prices are very reasonable.

New England is generally very safe for tourists, but never leave children unattended. Take care on the coast – the Atlantic Ocean can be very dangerous even on the most beautiful day. Take heed of all warning signs.

## CLIMATE

The best months for travelling in New England are generally from mid-May to mid-October. Many attractions outside the cities are only open during this period.

New England has very distinct seasons. The winter is very cold, with frequent snowfalls, but often blue skies. Spring is the season of maple syrup, with cold nights and fresh days. Summer is generally pleasantly warm but can be hot and humid. Autumn can be the best season of all, with sunny, crisp days and spectacular foliage. Vermont and New Hampshire have five seasons: the usual plus the Mud Season in April, after the snow and before the flowers!

## CONSULATES GENERAL

**Australia** 20 Beacon Street, Boston. Tel: (617) 542–8655.
**Canada** 3 Copley Place, Boston. Tel: (617) 262–3760.
**Ireland** 535 Boylston Street, Boston. Tel: (617) 267–9330.
**UK** 600 Atlantic Avenue, Boston. Tel: (617) 248–9555.

## CRIME

Crime is a very real problem but should be put into perspective. It is at its worst in the big cities, but no worse than many other major cities throughout the world.

General availability of handguns is one of the major problems, but the chances of even seeing a gun, other than on a policeman's hip, are very remote.

**Men's Suits**

| | UK | | | | | | |
|---|---|---|---|---|---|---|---|
| UK | 36 | 38 | 40 | 42 | 44 | 46 | 48 |
| Rest of Europe | 46 | 48 | 50 | 52 | 54 | 56 | 58 |
| US | 36 | 38 | 40 | 42 | 44 | 46 | 48 |

**Dress Sizes**

| | | | | | | |
|---|---|---|---|---|---|---|
| UK | 8 | 10 | 12 | 14 | 16 | 18 |
| France | 36 | 38 | 40 | 42 | 44 | 46 |
| Italy | 38 | 40 | 42 | 44 | 46 | 48 |
| Rest of Europe | 34 | 36 | 38 | 40 | 42 | 44 |
| US | 6 | 8 | 10 | 12 | 14 | 16 |

**Men's Shirts**

| | | | | | | | |
|---|---|---|---|---|---|---|---|
| UK | 14 | 14.5 | 15 | 15.5 | 16 | 16.5 | 17 |
| Rest of Europe | 36 | 37 | 38 | 39/40 | 41 | 42 | 43 |
| US | 14 | 14.5 | 15 | 15.5 | 16 | 16.5 | 17 |

**Men's Shoes**

| | | | | | | |
|---|---|---|---|---|---|---|
| UK | 7 | 7.5 | 8.5 | 9.5 | 10.5 | 11 |
| Rest of Europe | 41 | 42 | 43 | 44 | 45 | 46 |
| US | 8 | 8.5 | 9.5 | 10.5 | 11.5 | 12 |

**Women's Shoes**

| | | | | | | |
|---|---|---|---|---|---|---|
| UK | 4.5 | 5 | 5.5 | 6 | 6.5 | 7 |
| Rest of Europe | 38 | 38 | 39 | 39 | 40 | 41 |
| US | 6 | 6.5 | 7 | 7.5 | 8 | 8.5 |

**Conversion Table**

| FROM | TO | MULTIPLY BY |
|---|---|---|
| Inches | Centimetres | 2.54 |
| Feet | Metres | 0.3048 |
| Yards | Metres | 0.9144 |
| Miles | Kilometres | 1.6090 |
| Acres | Hectares | 0.4047 |
| Gallons | Litres | 4.5460 |
| Ounces | Grams | 28.35 |
| Pounds | Grams | 453.6 |
| Pounds | Kilograms | 0.4536 |
| Tons | Tonnes | 1.0160 |

To convert back, for example from centimetres to inches, divide by the number in the third column.

Most shootings are in areas that tourists would rarely visit. However, it is unwise to get into a confrontational situation with anyone, particularly while driving. Frayed tempers have often been known to result in shootings. Also, it is unwise to pick up hitch-hikers.

A more real problem is theft from cars and hotel rooms. Take sensible precautions and make sure valuables are not on display. Carry travellers' cheques, rather than cash. All hotels and most shops and restaurants accept US dollar cheques. Both Visa and American Express are widely recognised and provide fast service in the case of loss.

## CUSTOMS REGULATIONS

Everyone entering the US must pass through US Customs. Personal allowances for visitors includes 1 US quart (0.9464 litres) of spirits or wine, 300 cigarettes or 50 cigars, plus up to $100 worth of gifts. In practice, most of these items are far cheaper in the US than at airport duty-free shops, so there is little point importing them.

There is no restriction on the amount of currency imported or exported, but anything over $10,000 must be declared.

US Customs are particularly concerned about drugs, animals, meat (both fresh and processed), plants and fresh fruit. Penalties are severe.

## TRAVELLERS WITH DISABILITIES

The US is more alert to the needs of visitors with disabilities than many countries. Airports always have good facilities, including special lifts, toilets and wheelchairs. Most hotels, public buildings and museums have wheelchair access and toilet facilities. Always check

this before booking.

Handicapped parking areas, marked with a wheelchair symbol, are widely available, and hefty fines are levied for illegal use of these spaces.

Throughout New England people are sympathetic to the problems of people with disabilities and are generally very helpful. For specialised visitor information in Boston tel: (800) 462–5015.

## DRIVING

Drivers need a valid licence from any country that signed the 1949 Geneva Agreement. International Driver's Permits are generally unnecessary. Road signs use international symbols.

Major roads are well-surfaced and well-signed. In some rural areas there are sections of unpaved road. Motorways are called freeways and other main roads are highways. The speed limit on highways and freeways is 55mph unless otherwise posted. In town the limit is between 25 and 35mph. Speed limits are always well signposted and strictly enforced. On freeways you can theoretically be ticketed for driving too slowly in the left-hand lane, but this rarely, if ever, happens. The low speed limits mean that freeway driving is generally safe. In cities there is a continual problem with drivers antici-pating traffic lights or trying to make it through on amber. Always be careful at these junctions, as there is usually no delay phase in the lights.

There are many minor junctions where there is a stop sign in only one direction, and they are often not clearly marked. Pay particular attention when driving off the main roads.

If you have to drive in Boston, plan your journey ahead of time. Freeways can be so complicated that a missed turn-off can result in a lot of frustration.

New England is ideal for car touring and there is no shortage of petrol stations and garage facilities. For older cars there is one grade of leaded petrol (called gas, short for gasoline). For newer models which take unleaded (including all hire cars) there is regular and super, plus a recently introduced intermediate grade of 89 octane. Diesel is also available at most gas stations.

All gas stations have good maps for sale, and most car rental companies have local maps free of charge. The main motoring organisation in the US is the American Automobile Association (called the Triple A). The AAA has reciprocal agreements with overseas motoring organisations, and both roadside assistance and free route maps are available upon presentation of your membership card.

Avoid drink-driving at all costs. Keep any alcohol unopened and in the boot.

### Car hire

It is usually better to arrange for a car before arriving, using an arrangement such as the Thomas Cook brochure mentioned on page 180. Several airlines have special deals available with preferential rates if the booking is made in advance. Try to make a reservation as certain categories of car may be in short supply during peak holiday seasons.

Automatic transmission is standard in all rental cars. American cars are big, and a so-called mid-size is huge by European standards. The smallest size available is the sub-compact, which will just carry four people and a small amount of luggage. For summer travel, ask for a car with air conditioning, usually available at no extra cost.

None of the major car rental

companies will rent to anyone under the age of 25. It may be possible to find a local company that will, but be prepared to pay a loaded insurance premium.

If you hire a car, collision insurance, often called collision damage waiver or CDW, is normally offered by the hirer, and is usually compulsory. Check with your own motor insurers before you leave, as you may be covered by your normal policy. If not, CDW is payable locally and may be as much as 50 per cent of the hiring fee. Neither CDW nor your personal travel insurance will protect you for liability arising out of an accident in a hire car, eg if you damage another vehicle or injure someone. If you are likely to hire a car, you should obtain such extra cover, preferably from your travel agent or other insurer before departure.

### Breakdowns and accidents

In case of breakdown immediately inform the car rental company and await instructions. In case of accident:

1 Set up warning signs. Flares are usually used and are available from any auto store.

2 Call police and an ambulance if required. The emergency telephone number is 911.

3 Take the names and addresses of all involved, the make and licence plate number of the other vehicle, and the names and numbers of insurance policies.

4 Write down names and addresses of any witnesses, together with the time and date of the accident. If possible, take photographs of the accident from several angles.

5 Never, under any circumstances, admit to or sign any statement of responsibility.

## ELECTRICITY

The standard supply is 110 volts at 60 cycles. Flat two-pin plugs are used universally.

## EMERGENCY TELEPHONE NUMBERS

For police, fire and ambulance dial **911**. The Thomas Cook Worldwide Customer Promise offers free emergency assistance at any Thomas Cook Network location to travellers who have purchased their travel tickets at a Thomas Cook location. In addition, any MasterCard cardholder can use any of the Thomas Cook Network locations listed on page 186 to report loss or theft of their card and obtain an emergency card replacement, as a free service under the Thomas Cook MasterCard International Alliance.

Thomas Cook travellers' cheque refund is a 24-hour service. Report loss or theft within 24 hours, tel: (1–800) 223–7373 (toll-free).

MasterCard card replacement: (1–800) 307–7309 (toll-free).

## HEALTH

There are no mandatory vaccination requirements, and no vaccination recommendations other than to keep tetanus immunisation up to date. The standard of health care is extremely high, but so are the costs. It is essential to have a good insurance policy. Many doctors and hospitals refuse to give treatment without proof of insurance.

All major hospitals have 24-hour emergency rooms. Information on doctors and dentists can be obtained from hotels or listings in the Yellow Pages.

New England does not have many specific health problems. Tap water is obviously safe, but if hiking in the back country do not drink from the streams, as the water often carries the intestinal parasite giardia. A real problem is Lyme disease, which is contracted from ticks found in long grass.

AIDS is a continuing concern and, needless to say, suitable precautions are an absolute necessity.

## HITCH-HIKING

Hitch-hiking is only illegal on freeways. However, it is not recommended in New England. Motorists are very wary of hitch-hikers, and it can be very difficult to get lifts.

## INSURANCE

You should take out personal travel insurance before leaving, from your travel agent, tour operator or insurance company. It should give adequate cover for medical expenses, loss and theft, personal liability (but liability arising from motor accidents is not usually included – see under Car Hire, page 183) and cancellation expenses. Always read the conditions, any exclusions and details of cover, and check that the amount of cover is adequate. In particular, you should take into account the fact that medical treatment can be very expensive in the USA.

## LAUNDRY

All major hotels have one-day laundry and dry-cleaning services from Monday to Friday. Alternatively there are many dry cleaners offering a 2- to 4-hour service; check the Yellow Pages. Launderettes are also available.

## MAPS

General maps are available from car hire companies. More detailed town maps

A sign for all reasons in New Hampshire's Connecticut River Valley

and walking maps are usually available free of charge at chambers of commerce and visitor bureaux, which are listed in the Yellow Pages.

## MEASUREMENTS

America still uses the imperial system of measurement. The only difference is that the US gallon, quart and pint are 20 per cent smaller than the UK versions.

## MEDIA

The closest there is to a national daily newspaper in New England is the *Boston Globe*. Boston is also the home of the *Christian Science Monitor*, which is considered by many to be one of the world's most unbiased publications. In most towns you can find both the *Wall Street Journal* and the *New York Times*, which often give a more global view.

For local news, including weather and traffic conditions, keep the car radio tuned to one of the news stations.

In most parts of New England it is possible to receive a Public Broadcasting Service (PBS) station.

Virtually every hotel and motel room has a television. More often than not, it will be cable TV offering 30 channels or more. As with radio, there are usually two or three PBS stations; these give good news coverage, and most of the other programmes are British.

## MONEY MATTERS

Banking hours have traditionally been from 10am–3pm Monday to Friday, but competition in recent years has resulted in longer opening hours and even Saturday opening. There is no longer a general rule except the 10–3 core period is the same.

Travellers' cheques must be in US dollars. They are accepted in shops, hotels and restaurants. Many banks do not offer foreign exchange facilities, and most visitors exchange money at the airport or hotel. Thomas Cook MasterCard Travellers' Cheques free you from the hazards of having large amounts of cash, and in the event of loss or theft can quickly be refunded (see emergency telephone numbers, page 184).

Branches of Thomas Cook Foreign Exchange are listed below. All can offer emergency assistance in the case of loss or theft of Thomas Cook MasterCard

Chalking up the daily cruise details
in Nantucket Harbor

Travellers' Cheques. They also provide
full foreign exchange facilities and cash
travellers' cheques (free if commission in
the case of Thomas Cook MasterCard
Travellers' Cheques).
**Connecticut**
107 Broad Street, Stamford, tel: (203)
348–7725.
**Massachusetts**
160 Franklin Street, Boston, tel: (617)
695–0269.

If you need to transfer money quickly,
you can use the *MoneyGram* SM Money
Transfer service. For more details in the
UK, telephone Freephone 0800 897198.

All major credit cards are universally
accepted in New England.

Dollar bills are available in
denominations of 1, 5, 10, 20, 50 and
100. There is also a $2 bill, but it is
rarely seen. Although all bills are exactly
the same size and colour, the value is
clearly printed in each corner on both

sides. If you feel unsure, it is probably a
good idea to only carry bills in the lower
denominations to avoid any expensive
mistakes. Coins come in pennies (1
cent), nickels (5 cents), dimes (10
cents), quarters (25 cents) and 50-cent
pieces. It is always worth keeping a few
quarters handy for parking meters,
telephones and newspapers.

Sales tax is added to the price of all
goods and restaurant meals in New
England, with the sole exception of
New Hampshire, which has no sales
tax, but does tax meals and lodging.
Tax rates range from 4 to 7.5 per cent.
There are no restrictions on the amount
of money that can be brought into or
taken out of the US (see **Customs
Regulations**, page 182 for more
information).

**NATIONAL HOLIDAYS**
**New Year's Day** (1 January)
**Martin Luther King Day** (3rd
  Monday in January)
**Lincoln's Birthday** (12 February)
**Washington's Birthday** (3rd Monday
  in February)
**Memorial Day** (last Monday in May)
**Independence Day** (4 July)
**Labor Day** (1st Monday in September)
**Columbus Day** (2nd Monday in
  October)
**Veterans Day** (11 November)
**Thanksgiving** (4th Thursday in
  November)
**Christmas** (25 December).
**Patriots Day** is celebrated in
Massachusetts on the third Monday of
April.
Government offices, including post
offices, are closed for most of these
holidays, but few places observe them
all. Shops remain open on all but
Thanksgiving and Christmas.

## OPENING HOURS

Most larger shops are open seven days a week, typically from 10am to 6pm and from noon on Sundays. Smaller shops and more specialised businesses close on Sundays. Most offices, including government offices, open Monday to Friday 9am–5pm. Museums and art galleries vary dramatically. Recent budget deficits have resulted in severely curtailed opening hours at many state museums, so check before a visit.

## ORGANISED TOURS

The majority of people visiting New England hire cars, which is undoubtedly the best way to see the region. But particularly in cities, bus tours save parking headaches and ensure that nothing major is missed.

There are both ordinary and specialised bus tours available in Boston. If time is limited, an ordinary tour may fit the bill, but it will be fairly superficial and with a large busload of fellow tourists. Specialised tours cater for specific interests and are usually with smaller groups of people. Dozens of tour operators serve New England; hotels can usually give advice on what is available.

The widest range of sightseeing tours of Boston and New England are given by **Brush Hill** (tel: 800 343–1328), the largest operator of its type in the area. Tours are reliable and comprehensive but with large, impersonal groups.

**Specialised tours**
**Boston by Foot**, tel: (617) 367–2345;
**Concord Copters**, tel: (617) 247–3777;
**Old Town Trolley Tours**, tel: (617) 269–7010;
**Pitcairn Tours**, tel: (617) 696–8130.

## PHARMACIES

Most pharmacies are open from at least 9am until 6pm; many have longer hours. Drugstores have a pharmacy counter for dispensing prescriptions. Despite the name, drugstores are like mini-super-markets, with a wide range of products on sale. They are usually open until 9pm. The Yellow Pages gives a complete list of pharmacies. Many non-prescription drugs are available from supermarkets.

## PLACES OF WORSHIP

New England was founded on a strongly Protestant base, but today virtually every religion has a presence. Newspapers generally list times of services for the main denominations. A comprehensive list under 'Churches' in the Yellow Pages includes mosques and Buddhist temples; synagogues have their own listing.

## POLICE

Every incorporated city in New England has its own police force with normal police responsibilities including traffic control. For any emergency in New England, call 911.

## POST OFFICES

Post offices are generally open Monday to Friday 9am–5pm. They are always closed on Sundays. Post boxes, called mail boxes, are blue with 'US Mail' in white lettering. Stamps are available from vending machines in some hotels and shops, but they cost more than from a post office. Postage rates change frequently, so always check on current tariffs. An airmail letter or postcard takes about one week to travel from New England to Europe. Surface mail has been known to take 3 months! Parcels must be properly packaged and, if being sent by registered mail, non-removable, non-shiny tape must be used. Appropriate containers are sold at the post office. A Customs declaration form must accompany any parcel being mailed abroad.

*Post restante* is known as 'general delivery'. To collect you need some form of identification. Letters can be addressed to any post office and must include the zip code. Mail is held for only 30 days, after which it is returned to the sender, whose name and address must be on the envelope. Telegrams are sent from Western Union offices, not from post offices. If you have a credit card, you can dictate a telegram over the telephone and charge it. Western Union offices are listed in the Yellow Pages.

## PUBLIC TRANSPORT

The majority of New Englanders drive cars and, outside of Boston, the public transportation system is not well developed.

Local rail, metro (the T) and bus services in Boston are operated by MBTA over a very dense network. A main-line rail service connects Boston and Hyannis.

A network of long-distance buses, run by various companies, serves the whole of New England and provides connections to New York State and Canada. Full details and timetables can be found in the *Thomas Cook Overseas Timetable*, published bi-monthly and obtainable from branches of Thomas Cook, or by telephoning the order line on: (01733) 503571.

Greyhound is the major operator travelling between all the main cities. On some of the longer routes Greyhound is not significantly cheaper than the cheapest air ticket. For the greatest saving buy a Greyhound Ameripass, which is available for 7, 15 or 30 days and must be purchased outside the US.

In London the Greyhound office is at 14–16 Cockspur Street, SW1, tel: 0171–839 5591. Local offices in New England can be found in the Yellow Pages. Taxis are available in all towns of any size but are quite expensive.

## SENIOR CITIZENS

Most hotels, motels, restaurants and museums have preferential rates for senior citizens. Usually they want to see some form of identification, but often just looking old enough is sufficient – which can be very demoralising!

## SMOKING

Throughout the US smoking has declined so dramatically that smokers are very much the exception rather than the rule and are generally looked upon as social pariahs. Smoking is not allowed on public transport, in public buildings and in many workplaces. Hotels offer non-smoking rooms, and car hire companies offer smoke-free cars. Restaurants still have small smoking sections, but they are indeed small.

## TELEPHONES

Apart from telephone booths (kiosks) there are public telephones in most bars, restaurants, hotel lobbies and gas stations. All public telephones accept 5, 10 and 25-cent coins with 30 cents being the minimum charge. In airports there are often telephones that allow the call to be charged to a credit card.

Hotels usually charge a high premium for calls from the room. Conversely, some hotels allow local calls at no cost. Always check the rates.

Reverse-charge calls, 'collect calls', can be made from any telephone by calling the operator. Dial 0 for the local operator (00 for a long-distance operator).

The Thomas Cook Traveltalk card is an international pre-paid telephone card supported by 24-hour multi-lingual customer service. Available from Thomas Cook branches in the UK in £10 and £20 denominations, the card can be re-charged by calling the customer service unit and quoting your credit card number.

All numbers with an 800 or 1–800 prefix are toll-free. At a public telephone insert a dime first, which will be returned when you hang up. For international calls dial 011, the country code, then the number. The cheapest time for trans-atlantic calls is between 11pm and 7am. International codes are:

**Australia** 61;
**Canada** no code from US;
**Ireland** 353;
**New Zealand** 64;
**UK** 44.

Local directory information: **411**
Long-distance directory enquiries: dial relevant area code, then **555–1212**
Toll-free enquiries: **(800) 555–1212**.

## THOMAS COOK
See page 186 for details of Thomas Cook locations in New England.

Thomas Cook's World Wide Web site, at www.thomascook.com, provides up-to-the-minute details of Thomas Cook's travel and foreign money services.

## TIME
New England is on Eastern Standard Time, 5 hours behind GMT. Daylight saving time, when clocks go forward an hour, operates from the last Sunday in April to the first Sunday in October.

## TIPPING
Tips are a way of life, and everyone in the service industry expects them. They are very rarely included in the bill, except occasionally in restaurants. Always check. The amount is, of course, always at the discretion of the customer.

## TOILETS
Public toilets, called restrooms, are usually clean and free, but not always easy to find. In cities they can be found in department stores, bars, restaurants, and all gas stations.

## TOURIST OFFICES
For maps, comprehensive brochures and referrals to local chambers of commerce for more specific information.
**Connecticut Tourism Division**
Department of Economic Development
865 Brook Street, Rocky Hill CT.
06067. Tel: (800) 282–6863.
**Maine Publicity Bureau**
P.O. Box 2300, Hallowell, ME 04347.
Tel: (207) 623–0363.
**Massachusetts Office of Travel and Tourism**
100 Cambridge Street, Boston, MA
02202. Tel: (617) 727–3201.
**New Hampshire Office of Travel and Tourism**
Box 1856, Concord, NH 03302.
Tel: (603) 271–2665.
**Rhode Island Tourism Division**
1 West Exchange Street, Providence, RI
02903. Tel: (401) 222–2601.
**Vermont Travel Department**
134 State Street, Montpelier, VT
05602. Tel: (802) 828–3236.
**Discover New England**
P.O. Box 3809, Stowe, VT 05672.
Tel: (802) 253–2500.

## WHAT TO TAKE
Most people find that they take too much to New England. You can find everything you can get at home and more, and it is all cheaper.

## ACKNOWLEDGEMENTS

The Automobile Association wishes to thank the following organisations, libraries and photographers for their assistance in the preparation of this book.
**J ALLAN CASH PHOTOLIBRARY** 146, 147, 172; **MARY EVANS PICTURE LIBRARY** 10a, 11a, 72, 145; **MASSACHUSETTS OFFICE OF TRAVEL & TOURISM** 156 (Jennifer Lester), 163; **NATURE PHOTOGRAPHERS LTD** 140 (A J Cleave), 144/5 (P R Sterry), 145a (P R Sterry); **THE PRESERVATION SOCIETY OF NEWPORT COUNTY** 114; **THE RITZ CARLTON HOTEL, BOSTON** 173; **SPECTRUM COLOUR LIBRARY** 69, 73, 117; **ZEFA PICTURES** 7, 52.
The remaining photographs were taken by Robert Holmes.

The author would like to thank the following people and institutions for additional help: the state offices of tourism throughout New England, Maurice and Marjorie Holmes, his wife Bobbie and daughters Emma and Hannah.

The Automobile Association would also like to thank Ms Melissa Meehan, Thomas Cook Travel, Cambridge, Massachusetts for her help in the preparation of this book.

### CONTRIBUTORS
**Series adviser**: Melissa Shales       **Copy editor**: Penny Phenix       **Indexer**: Marie Lorimer
Thanks also to Robert Holmes for his updating work on this revised edition